The 3-Plan Retirement ™

Take Control of Your Finances and Retire More Comfortably

By

David Simpson

David Simpson

Dedication

This book is dedicated to the memory of Ralph Hahmann, who willingly shared with me his knowledge and experience about investing and encouraged me to do the same.

Acknowledgment

A mentor once told me that who we are at any point in time is the sum of all the things we've experienced leading up to that time. There have been lots of contributors, and given my age, some of the guides I remember most are no longer with us, but here are a few that stand out.

- My parents instilled most of the values that guide my life, but most importantly, the drive to be honest and fair with others, even if it hurts in the short term.

- My sisters – Charlotte, Laura and Cyndi – have always had a way of keeping me grounded.

- My teachers, especially Mr. Kagetsu, taught a bored overachiever that math could be both fun and useful!

- Mr. Stephen Wong, who presented a financial education seminar that allowed me to find a new direction for my life at a time when I desperately needed one, then gave me my first analytical tools to free my mind from what's really important.

- Ralph Hahmann, and his wife Lorna Davies, who always had time for my curiosity.

- Mutsumi, who inspired me to commit the time to make this long-imagined book real.

And finally, to my sons Mike and Andrew. Being a parent is the most difficult and rewarding thing I've ever done. I'm incredibly proud of each of you and hope you can be proud of this effort.

Foreword

In a recent poll, average Canadians thought they would need about $1.7 million to retire with a reasonable lifestyle. Your financial institution may quote a similar number to anyone asking the question, "How much do I need to retire?" In fact, it is probable that average Canadians got that number *from* their financial institutions.

But is this number the same for ALL Canadians? Does it apply to me?

In short, the answer is that you can have a very nice retirement with considerably less than this amount, but you need to be proactive in working with your financial institution because it's highly unlikely that that institution is being proactive in working for *your* wealth. This is *especially* true if you are already retired or will be retiring within the next 5 to 10 years.

This book is intended to explain, in simple terms, what you need to do, when to do it, and why you should do it so that you can take control of your retirement.

Why should you want to take control of your own finances?

Financial institutions are for-profit enterprises. Their objective is to make as much money as legally possible for their shareholders. Focusing on making money for their shareholders means they are NOT focused on making money for their customers. It IS a buyer-beware world, after all! The profits derived from servicing your account are significant. Wouldn't your life be better if YOU got more of that cash, rather than your financial "partner"?

So, if the idea of getting 50% to 75% more retirement cash flow each month from your savings is interesting to you, then this book will guide you on how to create the best financial future for yourself.

The book is divided into several parts. The first describes how the current system "works" for your financial institution and not for you.

In the second part of the book, we will review some basic investing concepts so that you can understand the ideas presented later. The topic of each chapter in this section is the title of the chapter. If you already know about the concept being discussed in the chapter, then feel free to skip it. However, surveys show that most Canadians don't really understand the operation of our financial system. The chapters are generally short, so you might want to at least skim through the material.

In the third part of the book, we look at how to arrange your financial resources to maximize your cash flow rather than your financial institutions' profits. We'll show you how the 3-Plan Retirement™ bypasses the restrictions your financial institution puts on their financial plan for you!

Here is our necessary legal disclaimer.

This book is educational in nature and is not to be taken as direct personal financial advice. Financial advice in Canada can only be provided by a professional, licensed in your province of residence, who is fully aware of your current financial situation, your attitudes towards risk, and your financial goals. While I am licensed, I am not your financial advisor – unless we have a signed agreement for me to perform that service. The intention of this book is to allow you to take more personal control of your financial future by having more informed discussions with your chosen professional.

Table of Contents

David Simpson

David Simpson

PART 1 – Canada's Financial System

Chapter 1
A Different Perspective on Retirement Planning

One of the most common questions people ask of their financial professional is, "When can I retire?" The answer is always that it depends.

There are several questions that these professionals ask to be able to calculate the "depends" for you, including:

- your desired lifestyle and the associated costs,
- your current financial resources,
- any pensions and probable government support,
- your anticipated life expectancy,
- the value of the estate you wish to leave to your beneficiaries,
- plans for travel,
- what emergency fund you want for unexpected expenses

In Canada, a recent study suggested that a household would need around $6000 a month, after taxes, to live a "reasonable" lifestyle – whatever that means. To have that level of monthly cash, you need an income of around $7800 monthly before taxes. You might be thinking that you don't need that much cash every month. Stay with us because you'll soon discover that even this amount won't be enough after enough time passes.

How will you fund this need for around $6000 in cash flow or $7800 in income?

That's why we are supposed to invest for our retirement.

Where do we invest?

David Simpson

Typically, Canadians invest at some of Canada's largest and most profitable firms. Those firms have Marketing Departments that work hard to attract your money.

Large financial firms know that we humans will come to a decision faster if there is fear involved rather than solely focusing on our hopes and dreams. This leads them to make interesting decisions in their approach to us, intending to maximize this potential fear. In this case, they make some assumptions about you.

These assumptions include:

- Uninformed customers prefer short-term results and either can't or won't properly consider the long-term.

- You believe that you must live only off the proceeds of your investments. Assuming you have no other income makes the requirement for the value of your investments larger! Needing to build a larger portfolio causes increased frustration, and many Canadians will give up even trying to build financial independence in retirement.

- Customers believe that their entire portfolio will generate the same return and that this return will not change every year.

- We evaluate risks in the long term to be the same risks that apply in the short-term, when there are many risks which only matter in the long-term. These risks can turn a good short-term low risk strategy into a much riskier long-term strategy.

- Most people believe that financial management is complex, requiring a lot of math! Those who believe this are more likely to follow the advice of any accessible "expert."

Marketing to these assumptions, financial institutions prefer to provide annuities in which the customer buys a guaranteed future cash flow at a predetermined monthly rate. The monthly rate provides an annual return of 5.5%. How much capital do we need to generate the $7800 monthly cashflow mentioned above?

The 3 – Plan Retirement TM

The answer is $1.7M. This is the target investment portfolio your favourite financial institution quotes to you.

At this point, many middle-aged Canadians start thinking, "I can never get there – without selling my house, and I don't want to do that!" And the fear starts to boil. Before our blood pressure rises too much, let's look at the assumptions.

The simplest assumption to break is the second one. This calculation ignores the money coming from the government (CPP, OAS, and GIS programs for seniors). While the payments from these programs differ based on your personal history, in general, they can provide approximately 20% of the required cash flow for a single person who has lived and worked in Canada for enough years, immediately lowering the retirement target to $1.36M. Feeling better yet?

For couples, there's a further reduction in the target to $1.02M from the partner's contributions from the government. The mountain to climb is now a lot shorter, but it's STILL a mountain to many Canadians!

What about the other 4 assumptions above?

That's why this book was written!

Education is the key to breaking these assumptions.

Before we start, a word of caution is needed.

The concepts discussed in this book are likely to challenge some ideas you may have always believed about becoming wealthy. Since you are reading an educational book, I'm assuming you are open to having a few of these ideas challenged. If not, put the book down, as you'll only be wasting your time.

Here's our first challenge.

In the mid-1990s, William Bengen, a now famous American financial advisor, developed a model demonstrating that a newly retired person could safely take 4.7% of his or her retirement capital in the first year of retirement, increasing the amount taken each year by the inflation rate, and would likely never run out of money in their lifetime, no matter how long.

That sounds promising – over the years, the income this model would generate is certainly an improvement on the cash flow from an annuity with a rate of 5.5% which never increases. (We'll see a more detailed explanation of annuities later in this book.)

But why was the rate set at 4.7%?

It's based on the recommended way that retirees "should" invest.

On January 3, 2023, the average annual return of the US stock market was just over 10%, as measured by the S&P 500 index. This is the average return per year since the S&P 500 index was established in 1957. The publishing date of this average annual return - Jan. 3, 2023 – was immediately after a very negative year for the markets. The average return published a year earlier was 11.88%, according to Investopedia. But we are going to use the lower return rate to illustrate a point.

Allow me to use some simple numbers to illustrate a key point.

If the goal for your portfolio is to provide the 4.7% Bengen suggested you should take every year, then this is equivalent to providing 37.6% over 8 years (4.7% per year times 8 years). Yes, there is inflation, which should change this math a bit, but allow me to keep this discussion simple for now.

With 37.6% of the portfolio used to cover the first 8 years, there's 62.4% left for longer-term needs. Let's invest this longer term 62.4% in the S&P 500 index at the reduced average rate achieved after 2022's down market. After 8 years, the 62.4% grows to be 133.8% of the original portfolio. If we use our long-term average inflation rate of 3%, the portfolio will need to have grown to 126.7% of the original payment to support Bengen's model of a 4.7% withdrawal for life.

This simplified investment approach shows a way to meet our future requirements without ANY return on the 37.6% portion of the current portfolio and no financial risk for the short-term cash flow!

What's The Implication Here?

The financial industry pushes models which serve to lower your expectations of what is possible. While it is important for those in this industry to be prudent in the projections we provide, the informed client should be able to understand the impact of our need to under promise to (hopefully) over-deliver.

In fact, the model to be presented later in this book will support a 7% total annual payout with a 3.5% inflation rate for a period of 27 years and 32 years at an inflation rate of 3%. Funding the original $78,000 annually, less government programs at a 7% payout would reduce the retirement funding target number to $750k from the 1.02M mentioned earlier. Now THAT'S significantly better than the $1.7 Million your favourite financial institution suggested as your savings target.

Is knowing that it is possible for you to have a reasonable retirement with a million dollars less than you're being told you need worth the time to explore a little further?

Then, let's push on with some background to help us understand how we got here.

Chapter 2
A Short History of Our Financial System

Many Canadians get all their financial services from one or just a few institutions. The major reason for this is that these institutions have branches at shopping malls and many large intersections in our cities and towns, which makes them very convenient. An additional reason we use them is that our parents trusted them. Since we trusted our parents, why wouldn't we also trust the same institutions that our parents trusted.

Our financial system has evolved over the years and bears only a small resemblance to the system we might have learned about when we were younger. We won't be discussing "why" the changes were made, as there's a lot of economics (things like economies of scale) and politics involved. But we will discuss how our financial system has changed since the days before President Nixon's decision to float the dollar versus gold, and the deregulation initiated by US President Ronald Reagan.

Shortly before the end of World War 2, a conference of the Allies in the New Hampshire town of Bretton Woods established new rules for the global financial system. The exchange rate system was set in place to facilitate global trade. Currencies were valued against a gold standard, and an explosion in international trade soon followed. This growth in global trade contributed significantly to the growth of the total global economy in the years following the war.

However, the limitation on currency values based on the supply of gold, along with the right to freely exchange any currency into gold, led to huge problems across the world as governments were ramping up spending to meet the rising demands of their citizens. In 1971, US President Nixon "temporarily" suspended American participation in the Bretton Woods agreement.

Allowing the value of the US Dollar to float against the price of gold allowed the government to print more money. At first, the strategy worked well, but then inflation kicked in, and by the end of the decade, inflation was over 14% in the US and higher in other countries. Up to this point in time, the best advice given to our parents was, "Get a good job, pay off your mortgage, then save some money, and you'll be fine." For the first 25 years after World War 2, this was a terrific strategy! But inflation changed the rules of the game. Most people never noticed the changed rules, and so never changed strategies. As a result, average families have been struggling financially ever since.

Prior to Reagan's deregulation efforts in the early 1980s, we had banks, trust companies, credit unions, investment brokers, mutual funds companies, insurance companies, all the same types of services we have now. However, at that time, each of those companies was independent of the others and provided independent advice and information. Our parents and grandparents could rely upon them, as those companies were required by their regulators to operate in a true customer-first manner and actually competed with each other for our savings.

Freed from the binds of regulation, the major banks started buying other financial services companies. Now, our largest banks have in-house trust operations investment brokerage agencies, and even offer some basic forms of insurance to further protect the banks from their debtors - you and me! These services were no longer subject to the regulators who had protected the consumer from abusive policies. Our sources of truly independent financial assistance have been dwindling ever since.

I remember, as a youngster, visiting a local branch of a major bank with my mother, who was helping her aunt organize herself after the death of my great uncle. Smitty had invested in 5-year bonds, with one-fifth of the bonds maturing every year. The plan was that Mabel would take the money she needed for the year and re-invest the rest in another 5-year bond for the future. The branch manager explained the concept to Mabel and my mother in such a way that eight-year-old me could understand, and we headed off satisfied that Mabel would be able to meet her cash flow needs for years to come.

It was simple, effective and easy to manage. One might even call it elegant. AND it worked!

However, I'm not sure that any financial institution would offer such a plan today.

"Bonds are way too risky, especially if interest rates climb! You want something more secure than that!" is likely what you'll hear today if you showed an investment professional from some financial institutions such an investment scheme.

It's natural for humans to dislike risk – it's how we survived as a species! If we were to be asked, "Which would you like, high risk or low?" the answer would always be, "Low, of course!" But we weren't asked the full question, and we were never exposed to the right knowledge to be able to answer the full question properly!

Let's start the discussion of risk by defining it. To me, 'risk' is anything that might increase the likelihood of an outcome that is different than the one I want. I want a comfortable retirement with enough health, family and friends to enjoy it. I'd like the freedom to travel from time to time and the ability to continue growing myself as a contributing member of society. Anything that would prevent me from achieving that goal represents a form of risk.

Risks can be found in many areas of life. Personal risks are found in the relationship, financial, health, physical and spiritual aspects of our lives. Externally, risks include global issues like wars, earthquakes, and climate change, as well as local issues like weather, fires, neighbours, etc. Obviously, this book is more concerned with understanding the sources of financial risk, and this chapter with understanding how the word "risk" came into our vocabulary in reference to financial assets.

What we now call risk in the financial area used to be known by another name – volatility. Volatility measures the responsiveness of an individual investment to news, which might affect the performance of that investment and the market in general. Usually, the higher the volatility, the larger the response is going to be to news – either good or bad. When the news is good, volatility is more our friend than our enemy. When the news is bad, volatility can hurt!

The 3 – Plan Retirement TM

Volatility is a (mostly) neutral word to us. We might wonder what it is if someone were to say the word in discussing financial investments. Risk is not a neutral word. We recoil at it every time we hear it!

So, why did our financial institutions stop using the word volatility when discussing financial concerns with us a couple of decades ago? The strategic reason is that they want to sell us low volatility products which make them more money – products whose return to us is ***guaranteed***, but only at a level ***far below*** what the financial institution will make from using the money we invest in these products in ways which produce virtually guaranteed returns over the longer term.

Product marketing is an interesting science. We are attracted to what we like, sometimes in a cautious way. If a stranger offers us $100, our first reaction is typically, "Sure, but what's the catch?" However, we are strongly repelled by things we fear – like snakes or darkness. The word 'risk' carries the burden of being such a fear.

So, our financial institutions decided that 'volatility' would become 'risk,' and we run to low risk versus higher risk. Do we really want lower volatility? Only if the returns generated when we invest at that proposed lower volatility level provide enough cash monthly for us to live the way we would like to live. More on that in the next chapter.

Think about marketing another way. If you were running your own company and had money to spend on advertising, would you advertise the products that make you the most money or those that make you the least? Of course, you would advertise the most profitable products. That's just common sense.

When you walk into your local bank branch there's an announcement board that also includes product advertising. Pay attention to what's being advertised!

In my branch, there are usually four things that are on those boards often. They are RRSPs, Guaranteed Investment Certificates (GICs), and TFSAs, usually with GICs in them, and pay off your mortgage early! These are what they WANT you to 'buy.' Do you know why? If not, then you are at risk of being financially manipulated!

David Simpson

Let's look first at why they want you to pay off your mortgage early. Suppose you bought a house today and needed a $1M dollar mortgage. Assume that the interest rate is 4.5% and that you want to pay off the mortgage in 25 years. You'll need to pay $5358.32 monthly for principal and interest. Over 25 years, you'll pay $1,667,496.

Banks have a limit on the amount of money they can lend out, based on the total savings and investments brought in from other customers. The lowest interest rates the banks earn on lending money are for money loaned to consumers in the form of mortgages and other fully collateralized loans. Other loan rates are higher. Some Canadian bank credit cards have 19.9% interest rates. If the bank loaned out the $1M in your mortgage in the form of credit card debt, and half that amount was paid off in full every month, then the bank would bring in $2,487,500 in interest charges over 25 years and would still have the $1M out on loan. Clearly, the bank makes a lot more money if you pay off your mortgage early.

What about you? Do you *want* to pay off your mortgage early? The answer depends upon your priorities. If you want to reduce your expenses as much as possible, then pay off the mortgage as quickly as possible. However, if your objective is to maximize your own wealth, then you might consider never paying off your mortgage!

Surprised? Most people are. Reducing expenses is only one way to get wealthier. Another way is to increase your income by increasing the total return on your assets. How?

The $5385.32 monthly payment includes $3750 as interest in the first month, with $1808.32 going to reduce the principle. In a standard mortgage, this reduction in principle reduces the amount of interest payable in the second month. But what if you don't pay down the principle?

What if you took the $1808.32 monthly and invested it, continuing to pay the $3750 monthly as interest. If your investment earned only 8%, then in 25 years, you would have $1,689,862 to pay off the $1 million mortgage, leaving you $689,862 further ahead. If your investments earned 10%, then you'd be $1,323,657 further ahead after 25 years. At 12%, you are $2,216,219 further ahead after the same 25 years. All this without paying a cent more than you would have if you paid down the mortgage the conventional way.

At this point, some readers will be thinking that the bank is looking out for their own interest in putting me in a conventional mortgage and then encouraging me to pay it off early. Exactly! The bank is supposed to make money for their shareholders, not for you! Ignorance can be VERY expensive!

We'll be looking at the RRSPs and GICs that the banks offer later in the book. TFSAs are long-term savings vehicles designed to allow you to earn capital gains, dividends and interest tax-free. It's like a high-performance race car when compared to other investing options available to most Canadians. Putting GIC investments into one's TFSA is like powering your racecar with an engine from an old Volkswagen Beetle – you're not getting the performance you deserve from the vehicle.

And What About Those Fees?

About 15 years ago, I sat down with the manager at the bank I was then using to ask the justification for the recent increase in the monthly fees the bank charged to small clients. He told me that the bank expects the branches to run profitably, so it seems reasonable that the users pay some sort of user fee. He told me that if I kept a minimum daily balance of at least $1500, my banking would be free.

I was always quick with math, so I used a conservative 12% return for the bank with my money and suggested that the bank wanted to make $180 a year off me to "pay" for the branch's services.

He did not confirm the number but left me with no doubt that I was in the right range. I then said, "You make more money off me from my credit card and my mortgage."

The answer? "Those profits belong to credit card operations and the mortgage department, not to the branch."

The conclusion from this story? The corporation owning the branches (for clarity, and only as an example, TD Bank Inc. owns TD Canada Trust Inc., which runs the branches for the bank) has segregated the profits from the business you provide them into divisions that are not compelled to help cover the cost of doing business with you. As a result, the branches are now deemed to be "unprofitable" and need to offset that "unprofitability" with fees for the services they perform!

I respect and admire the roles that banks have played in growing the Canadian, and more generally, the global, economy. But my personal belief is that in the time since deregulation, the spirit of our banks is not what it used to be – a source of independent advice on our financial strategies and futures. Now that the banks can (and do) own a variety of financial services, the branches which used to serve us well are now treated as low-cost gatherers of the financial resources (our deposits) which the bank needs to operate.

So, in this chapter, we've established that many familiar financial institutions are not operating in your best interest. You MUST be active in getting the most from your financial assets – especially as you approach or begin retirement!

Having established the need for you to be involved, we devote the next few chapters to giving you the background necessary to be able to discuss your options with a financial professional.

Chapter 3
Types of Retirement Funding Plans

Ultimately, there are two major categories of independent retirement funding options readily available to average Canadians – purchase of an annuity or withdrawing from a self-directed investment plan. Managed retirement preparation plans, such as company pension plans, deferred profit-sharing plans, and others are converted to one of these upon retirement.

TFSAs and unregistered accounts are essentially self-managed but can be converted into annuities at any time.

At the end of the year in which he or she turns 71, a Canadian must convert any remaining registered pension savings plans (RRSPs, Locked-In Retirement Accounts, Registered Pension Plans, etc.) into one of the two funding options, although the conversion can happen earlier.

It's important to understand all the risks involved in any investment decision, so we will invest considerable space in reviewing the types of risks for each type of investment.

Now, let's look at each of the two major investment options.

Annuities

Many Canadians choose to buy an annuity. Annuities provide guaranteed cash flow for life and are offered by insurance companies. In essence, an annuity involves you putting down a sizeable chunk of cash in return for monthly returns.

To buy an annuity, all you need to do is contact an insurance agent (never thought you'd actually WANT to contact one of those, did you?). I recommend an independent agent – one who is not contracted to one specific insurance company. Such an agent can search across companies for the offering which best fits your needs, while a "captive" agent can only offer you a selection of offerings from the insurance company to whom he or she is contracted.

14

How much does an annuity cost and provide? It depends upon the insurance company you choose, the guarantee period, as well as your age and sex.

Women tend to live longer than men, so the payout for an annuity for a woman is lower than the same initial deposit (called the "premium") would generate for a man.

You would prefer to buy an annuity from a larger insurance company, as the annuity is a guarantee from that insurance company to pay you every month for the rest of your life, so you want a company that will be around longer than you will! The tradeoff is that smaller companies offer higher returns, meaning more money in your pocket for taking on the higher risk. (As we saw in the previous chapter, higher financial returns are associated with higher financial risk levels.)

The guarantee period is the time after the purchase of the annuity for which your beneficiary would receive payments should you die prior to the end of the guarantee. As an example of this, if you purchase a 10-year guaranteed annuity and die at the end of year 8, your beneficiary will receive monthly payments for an additional 2 years. What happens to your money after that? It all goes to the insurance company! Your beneficiary gets nothing!

Using the online quotation system of a large company, we see that for a 65-year-old male wanting a minimum of 10 years guaranteed a $1M deposit into a non-registered annuity will receive $5739.91 per month at current rates. That's a return of 6.9% annually on your premium investment. The good news? This cash flow is GUARANTEED! There's certainly value in having certainty, but certainty always has associated costs!

We are about to discuss your implied costs for taking this guarantee – and those costs are significant! If, after finishing this chapter, you still are willing to pay the implied costs of this guarantee, then reading this book may not be a good use of your time, other than an academic exercise in understanding a bit more about how our financial system operates.

Let's look at the potential concerns you should consider when purchasing an annuity.

Inflation Risk

The monthly payment you are receiving is fixed. Usually, the amount is large enough at the start for you to live a nice lifestyle, but over time, inflation increases the cost of daily living. Assuming a future long-term average inflation rate of 3.5% means that prices will double in 20 years. At that time, your $5,739.91 monthly will have the current purchasing power of $2,869.95. Is that a risk you can accept?

Most people who live only on fixed pensions find that there comes a time when they can no longer afford to do the things they would like to do and that they must struggle even to live a regular life.

The lesson here is that if your assets are denominated in dollars (rather than shares, ounces, units or some other measure of non-monetary assets), then inflation is your biggest enemy. Don't ever think that inflation will go away! Build your retirement plan, taking inflation into account.

Capital Risk

This risk represents the possibility that you won't get your capital back from your investment in the annuity. In the example above, you put down $1M for monthly payments totaling just under $69k a year. At that rate, it will take 14.5 years for you to get all your capital back. If you don't live that long, you are relinquishing the rest of your capital to the insurer instead of to your beneficiaries.

Even the longest guarantee period - currently 10 years - does not cover this risk. If you die within the ten-year period, the insurance company will pay you, and then your beneficiary, a total of 69% of YOUR capital and none of the money they made from investing that capital!

Purchasing Power Risk

This is a combination of both inflation risk and capital risk. It's the time the elapses before you have received your full purchasing power of the original deposit back. In the example, this is 19.5 years. If you die before this time, then your family has lost absolute purchasing power.

Credit Risk

This is a measure of the possibility of the insurance company not being able to make the monthly payments before you depart this life. There are a variety of factors contributing to this risk, and almost all of them are tiny. All Canadian insurance companies are assigned a credit risk score by independent auditors. The lower the credit score, the higher the risk to you, and the greater the monthly payment you should receive. The larger the insurance company, the lower the credit rating is likely to be.

It's clear from this short summary that annuities are not as risk free as is suggested to us, although they are very low risk financially. Your independent financial professional can help you to create and evaluate potential scenarios based upon your desired lifestyle and your estimated lifespan.

Now let's look at the second retirement income investment option.

Self-Directed Plans

In a self-directed plan, the investor (either working independently or with a financial institution or independent advisor) chooses the investments in his or her plan. The investments allowed by the government to be put inside an RRSP or TFSA are limited – cash, stocks, bonds, mutual funds, Exchange Traded Funds (ETFs) also called Indexed Funds, GICs and other money market securities, and some covered options, which we will discuss in more detail in Part 2 of this book.

There are a few different risks inherent in many of these plans. The biggest one is the person from whom you get advice. A recent study concluded with the statement that "the average return for 20 years ending in 2015 was 8.2% for the S&P 500 index, while the average investor only earned 2.1%". Why the difference?

There are many causes for this difference, but the largest is investment discipline. Those individuals and organizations who make money in the stock market tend to buy when the market is down and sell when the market is high. Average investors do the opposite. Average investors try to time the market, while successful investors understand that it is time IN the market that determines long-term success. Average investors buy and sell based on emotion. Successful investors understand the true value of the companies in which they are invested, both now and projected into the future for 5 or more years. Buy and sell decisions are based on a process involving detailed evaluations of all current investment options.

So, what are the extra risks associated with Self-directed investing?

Market Risk

No one knows what the market will do tomorrow, as the news that typically drives the market hasn't happened yet. Even in the mid-term, predicting the next year is a challenge. Two recent examples illustrate this point. At the start of 2022, most investment analysts predicted a marginally positive year as the world continued to recover from the COVID pandemic. What actually happened in 2022? The markets (represented by the S&P 500 index) fell by 18.11%, the worst year since 2008! At the start of 2023, the same analysts were suggesting a slow and steady year of about 4-6% growth. By the end of 2023, the S&P 500 index was up 24.24%, recovering all the losses of the previous year.

A thought for newer investors to consider: there are ALWAYS people claiming the market is about to crash. I've been watching the markets for over 40 years, and it's always been the same. Many of these individuals loudly highlight the times they got their predictions right, without mentioning how often they were wrong. If you're considering using a newsletter that provides investment recommendations, choose one that tracks the results of every recommendation they've made. It's even better if each recommendation's performance is recorded based on the security's price two or three days after the advice is released. Some newsletters can influence the market for a security, especially with low- and medium-sized companies, when they suggest buying or selling it.

How can you reduce market risk? Invest for long-term gains instead of trying to guess next month's winners. The market always rises in the long term. More on this in the next section.

Security Selection Risk

Simply put, this risk poses one question: will you buy securities that rise over time? While markets generally rise, some securities inevitably lose value. Think of Nortel, Bre-X, WorldCom, Kodak, and others.

In discussing Market Risk, we highlighted that in 2023, the S&P 500 index fully recovered the value lost in 2022. However, this recovery was driven by a small number of stocks. Most of the 500 stocks in the index had not yet returned to their January 2022 levels by January 2024.

So, how does one go about picking the winners for the next year? The process may, or may not, involve looking at last year's winners, depending on economic conditions and other factors.

If we study the most successful investors, they tend to follow a few rules. The most common are:

1) Buy stocks you intend to hold for the longer term – typically 5 years or more.

2) Buy companies with a solid balance sheet.

3) Buy companies managed by people who have a track record of producing results for the investors who own the company, rather than for the management team which runs the company on behalf of the owners.

4) Buy companies who have a strong and sustainable competitive edge so that their competitors cannot easily catch up to their offerings and kill their sales. Anyone remember Kodak??

5) Buy companies whose stock price does not reflect your current evaluation of the book value of the company. The market often

overlooks good companies to focus on the industries currently in favour. This creates opportunities for patient investors.

6) Invest in at least 15 companies, but no more than 30. This strategy is called diversification. However, buying too many companies leads to over-diversification, which increases the likelihood that your portfolio's performance will mirror the overall index. Given the time and effort required to carefully select companies, your goal is likely to outperform the market, not simply match it.

IF you want these results, you should follow the process successful investors use. Keeping up with all the companies that interest you, whether as current or potential investments, can be a lot of work. If you don't have the time for independent research, it's worth considering paying for professional advice. This could come from multiple newsletters, a financial advisor, or a mutual fund manager. Another option is to invest in ETFs, as mentioned briefly above. These funds track the market, giving investors the same returns as the index being followed.

Some pundits claim that ETFs are the best option for the average investor. They often compare the returns of ETFs to the average returns of mutual funds that invest in the same index. In almost every case, ETFs outperform the average mutual fund. However, be cautious about putting too much stock in average numbers. After all, you don't want to be an average investor, do you?

There are many fund managers with long-term track records significantly better than their tracked index. The most famous of these is Berkshire Hathaway, which operates like a closed-end mutual fund. However, several other fund managers boast long-term track records of 15% and more. My personal frustrations with financial institutions began in 2006 when my branch-based advisor told me that I should be happy with the 6.5% return on my mutual funds from the previous year, as many people were getting less. I knew that numerous funds were achieving over 10% returns for that year, which I found frustrating. My chosen financial institution simply would not allow me to invest in the higher-performing funds, even when I asked for them by name after doing my own research!

Here I was, being told that I should be content with the inferior performance of the funds in which THEY would ALLOW me to invest MY money!

Put simply, if the growth portion of your investment portfolio has not averaged over 12% over the last 10 years, then talk to your advisor or consider changing advisors (and possibly institutions). This is not to say that your investment will grow by 12% or more every year; markets don't work that way. However, a good fund manager can be recognized by the returns they generate over a decade.

Market Timing Risk

Experts KNOW that they can't time the market. Those who have taken a few courses often become overconfident in their own expertise and think they can read the market. Statistics show that 90% of all people engaged in day trading (where the idea is to profit from market swings) do not make any profit at all! Those who do make money average around 15% per year. Between 1965 and 2022, the shares of Berkshire Hathaway (BH - Warren Buffett's company) have averaged compounded returns of 20% annually. BH uses a Buy and Hold strategy yet achieves better returns than most day traders!

In 2021, Bank of America published the following 100-year chart, showing the returns of the market for a decade leading up to the end of the year shown.

The difficulties of trying to time the market

Bank of America looked at the impact of missing the market's best and worst days each decade

Decade	Price return	Excluding worst 10 days per decade	Excluding best 10 days per decade	Excluding best/worst 10 days per decade
1930	-42%	39%	-79%	-50%
1940	35%	136%	-14%	51%
1950	257%	425%	167%	293%
1960	54%	107%	14%	54%
1970	17%	59%	-20%	8%
1980	227%	572%	108%	328%
1990	316%	526%	186%	330%
2000	-24%	57%	-62%	-21%
2010	190%	351%	95%	203%
2020	18%	125%	-33%	27%
Since 1930	**17,715%**	**3,793,787%**	**28%**	**27,213%**

Source: Bank of America, S&P 500 returns

What is most notable here is that, while money left in the market for 100 years generated an average of 5.3% compounded annually, if you missed the 10 best days in each decade, the average return is almost zero! Missing an average of only one day per year can have a huge impact on your investment performance!

While the impact of missing the 10 worst days is even more pronounced, predicting daily market performance is extremely difficult. Technology makes these predictions even harder, as the market is never the same as it was on any previous day.

For example, the most dramatic market day in my lifetime was October 19, 1987, known as Black Monday. At the bottom of that day, the Dow Jones (which was the most watched index at the time) had dropped 25% in less than a single day! While the causes of this drop are many and debatable, what is certain is that computer-based trading on behalf of "portfolio insurance" products offered at the time contributed significantly to the rapid decline.

The restrictions put in place have seemed to prevent a major collapse, but there have been hiccups. On May 6, 2010, the markets dropped over 7% in just a few minutes, caused by high-frequency trading generated by supercomputers at the brokerages on Wall Street. The restrictions (called circuit breakers) kicked in, and the market fully recovered by the end of the day.

Let's look at these events – very major on the day they occurred – from a longer term perspective. Here is a chart showing the S&P 500 index since January 1, 1959 to the present.

While it is possible to see the impact of Black Monday, over the longer term, a collapse of 33% of the market in a two-week period ending on Black Monday barely registers in this chart!

If you are investing for the long term, then you don't need to worry about timing the markets. Just pick good investments and hold them while the market recognizes the full value of the investments you've selected!

Addressing total Portfolio Risk

Reducing the risks or increasing the returns of your portfolio is a delicate task. There are only two successful approaches: either take the time to become and stay fully informed about your investments, or, if you feel your time is better used elsewhere, pay someone to do this for you.

How much time should you allot to staying informed? The people I know who are successful in self-selecting their investments typically spend four hours daily actively doing research. They also use one or two investment newsletters to help guide their research time.

My personal preference is to work with larger mutual fund companies that have enough staff to do the research necessary to outperform the market over the longer term. I also look for fund managers who follow the five rules discussed previously in the Security Selection Risk section. Most fund managers don't use all these rules, but they are critical to long-term successful investing. How do I find these funds? More on that when we discuss mutual funds in more detail later.

One final comment in this chapter: there are companies in the market that advertise, "Why pay the fund companies 2%+ every year to manage your money? Do it yourself and double your wealth over 30 years." This is a mathematically true statement—if you can achieve the performance of a well-managed fund over an extended period. BUT—and that but is HUGE—most people who succeed with this strategy find that they have a full-time occupation dedicated to market research and are also paying several services to provide data and external analyses to aid their own process. Almost everyone else generates very low returns from their portfolio.

In a research study published in 2015 in the *Annals of Economics and Finance*, Claude Montmarquette and Nathalie Viennot-Briot concluded that "over a 15-year period, accumulation has been found to be 2.73% to 4.2% per year higher for investors with a financial advisor." This figure accounts for all fees charged by the advisor and the funds used. Your advisor understands that returns are more significant than costs when it comes to creating your financial plan and outlook. The net returns for your portfolio are determined by total returns minus costs. Therefore, your focus should be on maximising the projected gross returns for the level of risk you are prepared to accept, as there is much greater potential for growth here than in merely trying to reduce costs.

PART 2
Investing Basics

This part of the book serves as an introduction to fundamental concepts and rules impacting investing. It is critical for the reader to understand these concepts, at least at a general level, to facilitate discussions with financial professionals and make more effective decisions about their financial plan.

No attempt is made to cover any of the concepts discussed in this part of the book in depth. Many of the topics overviewed can, and have been, developed into entire books dedicated to each individual topic. Instead, this book aims to provide enough information for you to understand why each topic is important and how, in general, it impacts your finances. We will leave the details of your specific situation for a discussion between you and your financial professional. After reading this section, that conversation should become clearer and more comprehensive than you currently believe you can handle.

Chapter 4
Do I have enough money?

Isn't this the real question we all want to answer!

I wish I could provide you with a simple yes or no answer, or even a specific number that guarantees a reasonable retirement lifestyle. However, those answers depend largely on you—your preferences, your lifestyle, and your ability to handle risk.

I would also like to say there's a very simple formula for determining how much you'll need. For example, if I have $500,000 for retirement and want to withdraw $3,000 per month without depleting my initial $500,000, my investments would need to earn $36k/$500k = 7.2% per year. That would be wonderful—if only it were that simple. But, investment returns can vary significantly from year to year, and can even be negative, so there must be some allowance for risk built into your plan as well!

What we can do is provide you with a method to determine how much money you'll need by the time you retire. This amount is often referred to as your Financial Independence Number (FIN). Based on your assumptions, you will be able to retire and enjoy the lifestyle you desire once you achieve this level of financial assets. However, to determine your FIN, you need to understand how your money should grow when you invest it.

So, we'll start there.

Understanding Investment Returns

When we invest our money, we want it to grow.

Sadly, this statement is not very specific. For example, what we truly want is to increase our purchasing power—we want to be able to buy more with the money we have in the future than we can buy now.

We know that inflation measures how the purchasing power of our dollars has decreased over time. If the Consumer Price Index increases by 3% in a year, then we would need $103 in a year to buy the same basket of goods we can purchase now for $100. If we had invested our $100 last year and received $103 this year, we would be no better off than we were last year—but we would also be no worse off, at least when considering only inflation.

Sadly, there are other considerations!

The most significant of these other considerations is taxes. The $3 you received above your initial cost of $100 is considered income. Both the federal and provincial governments will want their share. Additionally, your investment incurs various fees—after all, all financial service providers and institutions operate for profit. While you don't want to overpay for services, don't begrudge them their income. Would you work if your company weren't going to pay you?

Remaining in our current position requires that, over time, our investment return outpaces inflation, taxes, and the fees associated with our investment. Let's examine each of these five elements (time, return, inflation, taxes, and fees) in a bit more detail. For simplicity, we will discuss these in reverse order, as understanding time and return relies on comprehending the other elements in this list.

Fees

There are 4 major methods by which the person and institution providing your investments gets paid for helping you.

1) Account fees. These are usually an annual charge for having the account. For low dollar accounts the annual charge can significantly impact upon your actual return.

2) Transaction fees. These fees are typically charged whenever you buy or sell a security and can apply to both actions. A transaction charge incurred when buying is referred to as an Up-Front Commission, while a transaction charge when you sell the security is known as a Trailing Commission. Transaction fees can either be a fixed amount for each transaction, possibly increasing with the size of the transaction, or a percentage of the total

transaction value. The more assistance you require in managing your account and determining the investments you will hold, the larger the fees will be. For example, discount brokers, who offer no services other than facilitating the transaction, charge a low fee per transaction. In contrast, the fees for a full-service broker will be higher, as they provide access to research and expertise to help guide you in your investment decisions.

3) Management fees. Full-service brokers typically charge a percentage of the total assets in your account. This amount is quoted as an annual rate, usually applied monthly or quarterly. The fees are generally implemented either by withdrawing cash from your account, if available, or by selling a portion of some of the holdings within your account. Note that for brokers using this funding model, your investments are typically held in their name, and you authorize them to sell assets to cover these charges when you open your account. This type of account is known as a "nominee account.".

4) Trailers. Mutual fund managers need to be compensated for managing your money. They accomplish this by charging fees based on the total assets they manage and the number of transactions they execute in a given year. These fees are collected annually, and when aggregated across all the fund's units, they form the Management Expense Ratio (MER). The MER is the percentage of assets used to cover the fund's operating expenses for the previous full calendar year. For some classes of mutual funds (often referred to as Advisor Series), a portion of the MER is allocated to pay the professional managing your account. These payments are calculated as a percentage of the total investment, typically ranging between 0.5% and 1.0%.

Every financial institution establishes a combination of one or more of these charges to fund its operations and generate a profit. Expect any financial institution to readily inform you about which charges they do not apply, but ensure you understand all the charges in order to fairly compare your options. As with anything else, lower fees typically result in lower service, so you need to know in advance how much guidance you will require.

Taxes

Canada, along with all its provinces, employs a progressive taxation system. Progressive taxation means that the tax rate applied to your next dollar of income (known as your marginal tax rate) increases in steps based on income. Previously, provincial rates were calculated as a percentage of the federal rate; however, provincial priorities differ from one another and from those of the federal government. Now, the rates vary in each province. For the sake of understanding, we will use the federal tax as an example.

In 2023, the federal tax system consists of five levels. For the first $53,359 of taxable income, the federal tax rate is 15%. For the next $53,359, the rate increases to 20.5%. Progressive taxation means that the marginal tax rate rises depending on the income level into which your earnings fall. To clarify, if your taxable income is $53,358, the next dollar you earn would increase your total federal tax payable by 15 cents. The subsequent dollar would be taxed at the higher 20.5% rate, as your income has now crossed into that new level. The marginal rate applies only to the next dollar earned, not to all dollars earned!

Not all forms of income are treated equally. Capital gains are effectively taxed at half the rate of regular income. The government aims to reward individuals who invest, as investments drive the economy forward. Dividends also benefit from a reduced tax rate; this is because the company paying the dividend has already paid some tax on the profits that funded the dividend.

Investments can have different tax treatments, depending on the vehicle used to hold the investment. Taxes may be due in the year they are earned, deferred until funds are withdrawn from the investment, or deferred indefinitely. We'll discuss these aspects further in the next chapter. If your investment is in a tax-deferred (registered) account, you can ignore the impact of taxes on your existing investments. Many

Canadians misunderstand the RRSP offering, believing that taxes are deferred indefinitely. We'll also address this issue in the next chapter.

Inflation

Inflation measures the reduction in the value of the dollar, resulting in increased prices for the goods we need to live and enjoy life. As discussed in the preceding chapter, inflation is the enemy of anyone on a fixed income, often transforming what began as a very comfortable retirement into a significant challenge as we live longer! Recently, inflation has been hovering just over 2%, with a notable rise stemming from the COVID pandemic. Our long-term inflation rate, over the past 50+ years, is approximately 3.5%, which should serve as a reasonable figure to use in your financial planning.

Why do we experience inflation? Essentially, it occurs because we print more money each year than the growth of the economy can support. When we print more money in this manner, there is an increased amount of currency chasing the goods produced in the country, leading to higher prices.

Why do we print more money than the growth of the economy each year? Because our governments operate at a deficit, and those deficits need to be covered. This approach works for the government because it can provide all the services we demand while only including the interest on the accumulated debt in this year's budget. The repayment of the borrowed money has been deferred to the future, when it will be repaid in significantly deflated dollars. Additionally, the amount of debt individuals owe to financial institutions is increasing, contributing to the total fiscal deficit of a country as banks use leverage when lending money—more on this later, but essentially, banks 'create' up to 95% of the funds they lend when issuing a new mortgage.

To gain a better understanding of how the delayed repayment on government deficits operates, I recommend searching for a video titled "The Creature from Jekyll Island," which discusses the founding of the US Federal Reserve Bank and its role in our global financial system. One teaser: you'll discover that the Federal Reserve Bank is neither federal nor a reserve, and it's certainly not a bank. It's a unique creation that we all need to understand in order to grasp how our banking system generates substantial profits, regardless of how well the economy is performing.

Return

Return measures the amount of assets generated by your investments over the course of a year. Since we all have different sizes of investments, the return is typically expressed as a percentage. A 10% return on an account that started the year with a value of $500,000 means that the account's value at the end of the year is $550,000.

Obviously, higher returns are desirable. So why don't we all aim for the highest returns possible? The reason is that higher returns are usually associated with investments that have greater volatility. As we discussed in Chapter 2, volatility is one component of overall risk!

Sometimes, volatility can bite—hard! Many of us know people who had to delay their retirement after the 2008 market collapse because they had all their investments in the market, often in growth (higher-risk) stocks!

Time

In addition to return, the other critical element in growing your investment portfolio as much as possible is time. Many people underestimate the impact of time. A common mistake is failing to understand how the concept of compounding works.

If asked the question, "You have an investment of $100,000 that earns 10% a year. How much will it be worth in 10 years?" most people tend to calculate a $10,000 return per year, multiply that by 10, and conclude that the investment would be valued at $200,000 after 10 years. This answer is correct only for what is known as "simple interest." Simple interest pays a return solely on the initial investment.

The opposite of simple interest is known as compound interest, or compounding. Compounding indicates that the second year starts with a capital of $110,000, so a 10% return would yield $11,000 in the second year. The third year would return $12,100, the fourth $13,310, and so on. After 10 years, the investment would be worth $259,374! Clearly, compounding is a great advantage when it works in our favour!

But this sounds like it could get complicated quickly!

Surprisingly, the Greeks once considered problems like this one, and they uncovered a truth that humankind promptly forgot because it didn't seem practical at the time. This secret was later rediscovered by Albert Einstein, who was asked the question, "How can I know the time it takes for my investment to double?" The answer is incredibly simple.

Divide 72 by the return and you get the number of years it takes for an investment with that return to double!

At 4%, we would expect an investment to double in 18 years. At 6%, the doubling occurs in 12 years. At 8%, the doubling takes 9 years. At 10%, as in the example above, we expect it to double in 7.2 years.

This magical formula is known as the Rule of 72. It also works the other way! If I need my money to double in 8 years, I need a return of 72/8, or 9% a year.

Now, when someone says, "It's only an additional 2%! That's not important!" you'll be able to set them straight! You want every 2% you can get, as long as the volatility and total risk are acceptable!

How much does each dollar invested contribute towards achieving your FIN? We'll return to that after learning more details about managing personal taxes.

Chapter 5
Investment Vehicles

Several times in my career I've heard someone make a statement like, "I don't like TFSAs." This statement reflects a common misunderstanding of the nature of investing. To help clear up this misunderstanding, let's use an analogy - an automobile.

The performance of an automobile is affected by two primary factors. The first factor is the power in the drivetrain—let's say this is the engine of the car. The engine determines how much power the vehicle can transfer to the ground, influencing acceleration and, ultimately, forward speed. The second factor is the shape of the car, which determines how efficiently it cuts through the air. Sleeker vehicle designs reduce air resistance, allowing for faster speeds.

Switching back to your portfolio, the investments are the driving force behind performance, much like the engine! These investments drive the returns in your portfolio. You want the highest possible returns for the risks you're willing to take to achieve a better future.

The resistance working against your returns primarily comes from taxes, with smaller contributions from fees and commissions.

Here's the bad news for most Canadians—there's no reasonable way to avoid taxes unless you have a significant amount of money. However, you can reduce the impact of taxes to some extent. This book is not a detailed explanation of the tax system. There are accountants and lawyers who provide that service. Instead, our goal is to offer a general overview, so that you can consider tax implications when planning for your retirement.

There are several vehicles that affect how and when you or your estate pay taxes on your investments. These generally fall into three categories—pay taxes as you go, pay upfront, or deferred pay.

Prior to 1957, the Canadian tax system was relatively straightforward. Whatever money you received (income, interest, or dividends) was taxable in the year it was received. The only exception at that time was for capital gains, where all the income was deemed to be received upon the sale of the asset, with half of the increase in value being taxable. To complete a tax form, the taxpayer entered all sources of income, then subtracted all allowable deductions. The difference was taxable income, and all Canadians with that taxable income paid the same taxes. There was an income threshold (equivalent to around $18,000 in 2023) which was considered a basic living level. Incomes below this level were not taxed.

Unregistered, or "Open," investments are still mostly handled this way. These are the "pay as you go" vehicles. All other vehicles are plans registered with the federal government. We'll first look at the tax-deferred vehicles, using the RRSP as our main example, and then at pay-up-front vehicles such as TFSAs and permanent insurance.

RRSPs

In 1957, the Canadian government, having determined that Canadians were not saving enough for retirement, created a new tax incentive to encourage long-term savings. The Registered Retirement Savings Plan (RRSP) allowed individuals to "defer" taxes until a future time when they would no longer be working. If this were to be the taxpayer's only source of income, an amount up to the basic income level could be taken every year as tax-free income. While this wouldn't lead to a luxurious lifestyle, it provided at least a basic level of financial support.

The main benefit of deferring taxes was that it allowed people to save taxes by reducing their income during their higher-earning years, and then increasing their income during retirement, when their tax burden would be lower, or possibly zero. The benefit of an RRSP over its lifetime lies in the difference between the marginal tax rate when money is contributed to the RRSP and the marginal tax rate at which funds are withdrawn. The same benefit applies to other deferred tax programs offered to Canadians, notably the Registered Education Savings Plan (RESP) and the Registered Disability Savings Plan (RDSP). Both RESP and RDSP offer the added advantage of transferring income from the contributor to the beneficiary, who will almost certainly be in a lower tax bracket. If you have family members eligible for these plans, it's worth discussing with your advisor, especially if your income exceeds around $80,000 (the exact threshold varies by province).

So, what tax system changes have impacted the benefits of RRSPs since they were introduced in 1957? It turns out there have been several, and all have reduced the value of the RRSP for the average Canadian. The most significant change is that the basic living income is no longer tax-free, although a tax credit mitigates most of the impact for lower-income earners. Additionally, the government introduced a guaranteed minimum income for senior Canadians, ensuring that all citizens who have spent most of their adult lives in Canada will receive a basic living income through one of three government programs.

The net effect of these changes is that all money withdrawn from an RRSP (or its successor after age 71, the Retirement Income Fund) will be taxable at the lowest rate (currently 20.1%). Remember, the lifetime benefit of an RRSP is the difference between the tax rate on your next dollar of income when you contributed to the RRSP, and the equivalent marginal tax rate when you withdraw the money. Those who contribute to RRSPs while earning income at the lowest tax level will get NO benefit from their RRSP. Currently, all income below $53,359 is taxed at this lowest federal rate.

If your income is at the lowest taxation level, my personal recommendation is that you do not contribute to an RRSP. Similarly, if your income is in the second bracket (above $54,000 annually) but is growing and you have an aggressive retirement savings plan, I again recommend that you avoid contributing to your RRSP if you expect to have an income in the second bracket (around $4,500 per month) when you retire. In these situations, it's better to maximize your Tax-Free Savings Account (TFSA) —which we will discuss soon—before contributing to your RRSP.

Why would I make such a recommendation? There are several restrictions on investing and withdrawing money from a registered plan, and these limitations become more significant once you turn 71. You should be getting positive returns for taking on this level of risk, but unfortunately, many find themselves facing return-free risk! The same investments held outside your RRSP will generate the same after-tax monthly cash flow if used to purchase an annuity with the fund's contents at retirement. So, the net result is that you have restricted access to your money, yet no increase in after-tax cash flow to justify the loss of flexibility.

With an income at the third taxation level or higher – currently $106,719 – an RRSP is a very sensible investment, once TFSA contributions have been maximized.

TFSAs

The Tax-Free Savings Account (TFSA) was introduced in the 2008 federal budget and came into effect on January 1, 2009. Prior to its introduction, the concept was outlined in a federal discussion paper, where it was referred to as the Tax-Free Investment Account. The concept was well received, gaining support from the Canadian Taxpayers Association and all Canadian financial institutions, who only requested a slight name change.

The TFSA allows Canadians to deposit after-tax dollars (this type of vehicle is referred to as a "pay up front" model). These funds can then be withdrawn from the plan on a tax-free basis for any purpose, without any age or income restrictions. The major benefit is that all growth generated by the investments is also received tax-free! However, the concern with how most Canadians invest their TFSA money is that they tend to buy guaranteed investments with low returns, which don't generate enough benefit to make the program worthwhile. No growth equals no benefit!

Why would someone take a high-performance vehicle like the TFSA and put a ridiculously underpowered engine in it? It's all in the name. Most Canadians view the TFSA as a tax-free savings vehicle rather than a tax-free investment vehicle. Big mistake!

As a true investment vehicle, the TFSA is a total gift for every Canadian. It's a terrific way to save for major purchases, as well as for retirement. How good is it?

For a 32-year-old planning to retire at 67, earning $47,000 a year (in the lowest tax bracket) but able to invest $6,000 a year towards a better future, the TFSA will generate 22.9% more after-tax cash flow than an RRSP, assuming the tax return is not invested. This 22.9% extra is `higher than the 20.8% tax savings from contributing to an RRSP, so from a pure long-term perspective, it makes no sense to put money into an RRSP at this taxation level.

The benefit changes with increasing tax brackets, so it's good advice to consult with an independent financial planner.

Permanent Insurance

Insurance is one of the real secrets used by the wealthy to generate cash flow without paying taxes. The less wealthy? We often hear, "You don't want insurance! It only pays when you die!" Interestingly, we usually hear this from institutions that cannot sell us insurance. In the financial arena, only take advice from people who are licensed to discuss the options they present, as there are ethical conduct rules to protect you from intentionally poor advice.

This section is only a brief overview of insurance. The topic is the subject of many books. Rather than reading them all, I recommend speaking to a licensed insurance agent if the concepts presented here interest you.

In Canada, there are three major types of insurance: term, whole life, and universal life. They are intended for different uses.

1. Term – term insurance is the lowest priced form of insurance. It lasts for a preset period, then expires. The term can be from 10 to 30 years, depending upon the insurer. Term is best used to cover short term risks, like mortgages, or when more expensive types of insurance are not affordable.

2. Whole Life – The original type of permanent insurance is called Whole Life. In this type of policy, the insurer invests the extra

premium on behalf of the policy owner. The returns on this investment are guaranteed for the life of the policy and are usually in the 4-5% range. "Participating" policies add an extra annual "dividend" payment based on the profitability of the company. Typically, the total return of participating policies is in the 5-7% range. Whole Life is a great option for corporate uses, for specific purposes (for example, as additional savings for children's education), when protecting a large sum of money, and for people who don't want the risks inherent in Universal Life policies.

3. Universal Life – In response to clients concerned about the lower long-term returns of Whole Life policies, the insurance industry created a new policy type. For those willing to take on market risk, the Universal Life policy allows the policy owner to make all investment decisions. While the investment choices include some guaranteed options, the returns on these are usually lower than the guaranteed returns in a Whole Life policy. Good Universal Life investments include market ETFs and growth mutual funds, as these policies should be considered long-term investments.

One of the benefits of permanent insurance is that it can be used to generate retirement cash flow. An Insured Retirement Plan (IRP) involves borrowing monthly against the policy using a collateralized loan from an independent financial institution, other than the insurance company that offered the policy. Since the policy owner is borrowing against an asset, the monthly cash is not considered income, making it entirely tax-free! This concept is similar to having a reverse mortgage on a house. There are no monthly payments on the loan, which will be paid off—tax-free—by the insurance company when the insured person passes away.

In my experience, when comparing TFSA payments to those of a Universal Life policy with the same assumed investments, the Universal Life plan typically provides 20% more than the TFSA investments for policies in place for 30 years or more! Most of my clients who started with me before turning 35 are investing equally between a TFSA and a Universal Life policy. An excellent combination!

For the Math Geeks

In my practice, I use spreadsheets to allow prospective clients to see how a variety of variables and decisions can affect their future cash flow. For those who aren't likely to develop their own spreadsheets, you can skip these calculations entirely without losing any of the key insights of this book.

As promised in an earlier chapter, here are the formulas for calculating the impact of an investment on reaching the Financial Independence Number (FIN), allowing you to retire. Note from the equations that, for the same dollar value in an RRSP and a TFSA, the TFSA will provide more after-tax cash flow than the RRSP by an amount determined by your marginal tax rate at the time you withdraw the funds. As we saw in the discussion of taxes above, this rate will be at least 20.8% (the minimum Federal Tax Rate).

The impact is different depending on which of the three tax treatment types mentioned earlier are being used.

To calculate the impact of any new investment on achieving your FIN, use the following formula for tax exempt investments (such as a TFSA):

Impact = Investment x ((1+return) ^ (years invested))

where the ^ character represents the "raised to the power of" operator, and

(1+return) is the multiplier for growth in any year

(10% growth is the same as multiplying the capital by 1.10)

For tax deferred investments (RRSP, RDSP, etc.) we must consider the taxes to be lost when we withdraw the money from the registered account. The equation becomes:

Impact = (Investment x ((1+return) ^ (years invested))) x (1-marginal tax rate)

The 3 – Plan Retirement TM

Where the (1 - marginal tax rate) shows what will be left after taxes are deducted from withdrawals spread over the years. The rate used should be a combination of federal and provincial tax rates based on your income level.

For unregistered investments, we assume that you have invested solely for capital gains. The capital gain is the final amount minus the initial amount. The tax rate will be the marginal tax rate from above, divided by 2. The tax-due equation becomes:

Taxes = (Investment x (((1+return) ^ (years invested))-1)) x (1-marginal tax rate/2) and

Impact = Investment x ((1+return) ^ (years invested)) - Taxes

Chapter 6
Establishing Your Retirement Financial Plan

Before we start this chapter, a bit of context is required.

This chapter has been developed through my own interactions with the Canadian banking industry over the past 55 years. The primary focus of this chapter will be on these banks – to whom the majority of lower- to middle-income Canadians turn for financial advice and products. I have also confirmed that the information in this chapter is still current through discussions with former bank employees, including those who left through retirement or either voluntary or involuntary career changes.

One of the truest sayings I learned in my business career is: "If you know how a person is measured, you know how that person will behave." We are going to look at how the people from whom most of us get our financial products and information are measured. Not every bank measures their people in exactly the way we will describe, but most of them are similar to the generic "bank" described in this chapter. Please feel free to discuss the concepts you will read about here with your branch manager, but be prepared for the possibility that he or she may not want to openly discuss some of the items mentioned. If you do not know how your branch manager is incentivized, your ability to deal effectively with your branch will be reduced.

Now, let's talk about your retirement plan and how it works within a bank branch. Again, this is where most Canadians have their retirement funds. These institutions have their own rules for how clients can invest with them. Rules are typically a good thing in the financial services industry, as they prevent many errors and problems from occurring. Typically, the differentiators between the larger banks are determined by internal (i.e., marketing) rules, not by rules set by regulators. Some of these rules can pose significant problems for you.

A typical rule is that each person is allowed only one plan. Another rule segments the consumer market based on your wealth. Finally, there is the incentive for branch managers to drive the lowest possible cost of capital to increase their likelihood of being promoted to district manager. There are many other rules, but these three are the most impactful to the topic of this book.

Let's look at the implications of these internal rules in more detail.

Promotion Requires Low Capital Costs

The banking industry, like many other industries, is a highly competitive place to work. Many people are vying for a few promotions, and the difference between getting a big promotion and missing out is often small. The numbers your team produces matter immensely in your evaluations.

One key result area for a bank branch that matters in our discussion is the branch's ability to efficiently and effectively raise funds for use by other departments or companies within the bank's corporate structure. In this particular result area, there are two main numbers.

The first number is the total capital the branch raises. This can be viewed as the sum of all savings, checking, and current accounts at the branch, as well as the sum of all investments sold by the branch. These investments include GICs, money market accounts, investment "portfolios," and a variety of mutual funds. When these two are combined in a weighted sum, the branch's capital generation effectiveness is measured.

The second number typically provides an average costing rate for the capital brought in by the branch. This one's a bit more complicated.

The bank exists to make profits for its shareholders. Therefore, the efficiency measurement attempts to calculate the average annual "cost" to the bank for the funds the branch has acquired. Cash account deposits are not very efficient, as the bank must keep a percentage of this money available to cover withdrawals. This coverage money earns very little for the bank, so banks prefer to move your money into their investment side.

Anyone whose savings or checking accounts grow to a reasonable size has likely been asked by the Customer Service Representative (CSR –

previously known as tellers when the branches only handled banking) if they would like to earn more interest on their money by buying a guaranteed investment certificate (GIC). CSRs only sell two products in the modern branch – GICs and credit cards – both of which are highly profitable for the bank. One of the critical performance measures for CSRs is how many of each of these they sell monthly, and there is a lot of pressure on CSRs to sell or leave the bank. CSRs can also achieve positive results from referring customers to the investment side of the business, especially if they cannot close a sale on a GIC.

Once you get to the investment side, the level of customer service doesn't increase significantly. Typically, you'll be given an appointment with an investment "specialist." In too many branches, the only "specialty" that person has is a short training course on how to operate the computer system, which is responsible for making the recommendations that you will be offered during your 12-to-13-minute meeting. I was shocked when, after meeting a person who provides this training within one major bank, they confirmed that the expectation is for the specialist to process each client within this very short period of time.

When I personally went through this process for the third time (in 2005), I took note of the questions I was asked. They included a few questions to assess my attitude towards risk.

The situation was that I had recently received a $50,000 bonus cheque, had done my own research, and went to a major bank with a list of five funds in which I wanted to invest $10,000 each. The funds I had selected were among the top performers offered by the bank's mutual funds affiliate. Two of them were categorized as High-Risk, two as Medium High, and one as Medium-Risk. I indicated that I understood what the categories meant and that I was prepared to accept the volatility implied by the High-Risk rating.

Despite this self-evaluation, the risk profile rating I received at my branch was Medium High. I directed the specialist to override that setting. Lower risk profiles mean less risky investments, which provide lower returns and therefore keep the branch's "cost of capital raised" lower.

The 3 – Plan Retirement TM

I was asked if I knew where I wanted to invest my money, referring to global markets, market segments, investment types, etc. A reply of "No" to this question would result in an offer to invest your money in a "portfolio" of mutual funds. I was told that all the funds were 3- and 4-star funds. The funds I had researched were all 5-star funds – the highest rating. I declined the offer to "help" me invest in the right places.

In later years, when asked by a client, I checked out these portfolios in more detail. Each "portfolio" invested in a set of the bank's other mutual funds. While each fund did show as either 3 or 4 stars, when I checked into each fund, I found that they were a different version of the funds than those available to investors. The funds each had a Management Expense Ratio (MER) of 0.08%. The version of these funds available directly had an MER of around 1.4% if your advisor charges a fee for managing your account, or 2.4% if they don't charge you directly. When I checked the version of these funds that were generally available, I found that each of them was a 2- or 3-star fund, and that almost all the funds were less than 5 years old.

To outperform the market using mutual funds, we should be buying only 4- and 5-star funds, which achieve that rating by having superior performance over 5 and 10 years! Most independent advisors will not sell a fund that doesn't have a long-term track record, unless they know the manager of the fund and that person has an excellent track record. None of these funds – not a single one! – qualified under these criteria. There wasn't a single fund in any of the portfolios that I would have sold independently!

All the generally available versions of the funds had underperformed their market by 3% or more! I was prepared to accept that the reduction from 2.4% MERs to 0.08% would cover much of this difference, but the portfolio also charged a fee, which turned out to be 3.02%! A typical bank has over 100 of these portfolios. I found that all these funds were "managed" by 2 people, who on average couldn't devote more than 25 minutes of attention to each fund every week!

A few years later, I repeated this analysis for another bank. At the time, that bank had 121 portfolios, again managed by 2 people. The results were identical – all 2- and 3-star funds, repackaged to look like 3- and 4-star funds. All were too young for independent advisors, and all were significantly underperforming the market!

Finally, while this book was out for review, one of my clients was switching her accounts to follow the 3-Plan Retirement™ model. She had her short-term funds invested in GICs at a large bank, and her long-term funds with me. As she will be retiring in 2-3 years, it was time to set up her mid-term fund investments. She called me to set up an appointment, having already arranged one with the bank.

I coached her to approach the bank as follows: "This is money that I don't plan to use for 5 years or more. I will not be making a final investment decision for a few weeks, but I'd like to know what you can offer me."

What the bank offered were 2 portfolios, both medium-low risk, which is entirely appropriate for this client. However, the 5/10-year returns on the two funds were 5.69% / 4.67% for the balanced growth portfolio and 2.69% / 2.73% for the balanced income portfolio.

Why so low?

That question is ALWAYS answered by looking at the investments within the portfolio. Both portfolios have, as their top investment, one of the bank's bond funds. That investment constitutes almost 33% of the value of the balanced growth portfolio and over 41% of the balanced income portfolio. When I looked up that fund, the 5-year performance was negative, averaging -0.43%! To be clear, the fund has lost that amount each year, so an initial $10,000 investment in the bond fund is now worth $9,877. It's been a challenging time for bond funds, which is usually the case when interest rates are rising, so I didn't expect much.

However, over the same period, the index of the bond market rose an average of 0.21%. This fund underperformed its index by 0.64% per year. Not surprisingly, this makes it the worst-performing bond fund available from the bank. What DID surprise me is that it's the LARGEST of the bank's bond funds, with well over $20 million invested – nearly 4 times the size of the next largest Canadian bond fund available from the bank. Who puts their money into a poorly performing fund?

I checked the 11 largest portfolios available through the bank and its affiliates. Over 67% of the money in the poorly performing bond fund comes from these 11 portfolios!

No one should be amazed that the fund has had 2 manager changes in the past 5 years! It's being kept afloat by the bank's retail customers, who are supporting underperforming management, but have little visibility into that information.

The stock components of the two portfolios are mostly underperforming funds as well, with 2 exceptions.

In summary, the appearance is that portfolios are what the banks have been using to provide funds for newer or developing fund managers. Those funds that perform well move out of the portfolios and into other channels. Those that don't perform well are closed, and your money is moved into another fund development "experiment"! On average, these portfolios underperform their benchmarks by over 4% – not a good place for you to put your money.

Why do the banks put you here? Incentives! Portfolios are a low-return, high-profit investment model, carrying the highest profit and lowest cost of capital of all the market-based investment options available through the branch.

Buyer beware!

One Customer, One Plan

When we invest our money, we want it to grow. The banks also want it to grow – but they want more of it to be growing on their behalf! That happens when the bank can limit your returns on the investments you make.

Limiting your returns is easy! Determine the investment objective that leads to the lowest investment risk level, then invest ALL your money at that level.

If you need to use a portion of your money within a few years, then the industry regulators mandate that your plan must be low risk, or possibly low-medium risk. Typically, your financial institution will suggest you invest in something called Guaranteed Investment Certificates (GICs). As this book is being written, the best available rate for a 5-year GIC from a major Canadian bank is 4.35%. As we saw previously, this rate means that putting $100,000 into a 5-year GIC would result in interest earnings of $4,350 each year.

What do banks do with your GICs? They use them to fund mortgages. Five-year GICs fund five-year mortgages. Currently, the best rate for a five-year conventional mortgage is 5.74%. You might draw the conclusion that the bank makes about 1.4% from your GIC, since 5.74% – 4.35% equals 1.39%. If you think this, then your math is excellent, but you don't understand how banks operate!

Banks have special rules that only apply to banks, allowing them to make money in ways not permitted for any other type of corporation or person. The most significant of these rules is the concept of fractional banking. Depending on how secure the sources and uses of money are for the bank, they can lend out far more money than they take in.

Because your 5-year GIC investment is locked in, these funds are guaranteed to be available to the bank. The bank knows exactly how much it will have to pay and precisely when it will pay it. The mortgage, similarly, is virtually guaranteed. Defaulting on a mortgage can cost you your house, which is usually worth far more than the mortgage. The bank knows that the mortgage payments will be made for almost every mortgage it issues.

Because these cash flows pose very little risk to the bank, banks can use a 5% fractional banking rule for this GIC and mortgage combination. This rule means the bank must keep assets worth 5% of the value of the mortgage. Put another way, your $100,000 GIC effectively backstops $2,000,000 in 5-year mortgages!

You might ask, "Where did the other $1,900,000 come from for that mortgage?" Great question – and one with an astonishing answer! The bank is allowed to create the $1,900,000 out of thin air when it issues the mortgage! They're making money by lending the mortgagee money the bank didn't even have! So how well does this work for the bank? Let's break it down!

At 5.74%, this $2,000,000 5-year mortgage generates $114,800 in interest income for the bank each year. The bank's only cost for this mortgage is the $4,350 it paid for your GIC. In summary, at the given rates, the bank makes a gross profit of $110,450 per year for every 5-year $100,000 GIC it sells – an annual gross profit rate of 110.4%!

Wouldn't you like to be in the banking business? Is it any wonder that these financial institutions want as much of your money in Low Risk as they can possibly convince you to give them?

How does that impact your cash flow in retirement?

Well, if you invested $1,000,000 in GICs at the rate we used here, you would earn $43,500 annually, or $3,625 monthly, without using up your initial capital. You could live forever and continue to withdraw that amount!

If you wanted to take a fixed $5,000 monthly, your cash would run out in 29 years, with you receiving a total of $1.74M over that time. During this period, the bank has generated a gross profit of $18.7M directly from your money, and you are now penniless! Since the bank reinvests the profit they generated, the actual total amount they make from your retirement funds is much higher than the $18.7M directly earned from the mortgages you funded.

Worse yet, the fixed monthly withdrawal of $5,000 leaves you exposed to inflation risk. In 29 years, at the current long-term average inflation rate of 3.5%, the $5,000 monthly will buy what $1,843.75 buys now!

In summary, this plan exposes you to many risks, including, but not limited to, inflation risk, money risk (the chance that the government will devalue our currency), capital risk (you lose ALL yours), and the risk of running out of money!

Does *any* of this seem fair to you? Me, neither!

Market Segmentation

Let's return to my $50,000 investment mentioned earlier. The situation was that I had recently received a $50,000 bonus cheque, had done my own research, and went to a major bank with a list of 5 funds in which I wanted to invest $10,000 each. What happened that day is the major reason I decided to enter the financial services industry, with a focus on education! I remember it like it happened yesterday!

Once my risk profile was manually adjusted, the licensed wealth specialist with whom I was working entered my investment preferences into the computer that determines which investments I would be allowed to make.

"I can only give you one of your funds!"

It turned out that one of the funds I requested was a fund specializing in investments in the Far East. As the bank only had one of those, they offered it to me.

"What about the others I wanted?"

"Those funds are closed to you. But don't worry, I have other funds just like them."

And so, I ended up with four funds that I hadn't researched, all of which underperformed the funds I had actually requested! Why? Let's unpack this short conversation.

In the mutual fund industry, a fund chooses to become closed when the fund manager does not want to take in additional money. Many successful funds have taken this step. It's a challenge for a fund that gets too large to outperform the market! So, I interpreted the comment as "Those funds are closed," ignoring the "to you" part.

I found out later that the funds were not closed at all. In fact, they were only closed to me trying to buy them through my branch!

I was an unintentional and uniformed victim of market segmentation!

Essentially, the bank knows that the best funds will lose their competitive edge if the fund becomes too large. That's why some funds need to "close" themselves to new investments. Like any other company, the banks want to provide the best results to their best customers so they won't lose them to competitors!

With my increased home equity and a dwindling home mortgage plus the total amount I had previously invested, the new deposit wasn't enough to entitle me to "best customer" status. Instead, I was offered the third-tier funds in each of the categories I had requested!

What do I mean by third tier?

Most banks have 2,000 or more mutual funds. There are simply not 2,000 different categories of investments from which to choose, so there's a lot of overlap between funds. The funds that generate the best returns naturally attract the most money. These funds get first choice for the investments they select. Lower-performing funds get their pick of the investments left over after the higher-performing funds make their decisions.

A bank may choose to limit the possible investments of lower performing funds for several reasons. These include, but are not limited to:

- Not wanting to have too much money invested in any one security.

- Not wanting to reduce the total amount of a security in general circulation.

- Wanting to build their relationship with client companies who have the potential to grow in the future.

- Achieving a political aim.

If it seems to you that some of these reasons have nothing to do with whether or not the company is a good investment for your money, then you're beginning to understand why most of us do not get the investment performance we deserve.

One year after my $50,000 investment, I returned to the wealth advisor to complain. The market had gone up more than 8% in the preceding year, while the four funds I was given had returned around 6.7%. This time, I received another highly memorable answer!

"You got 6.7% and you're complaining? You should be ecstatic! Most people got 4 to 5%!"

The message was clear to me. My branch will provide me with inferior products and tell me to be grateful for whatever return they manage to achieve!

I stopped using the bank for investments. I advise you to do likewise!

Chapter 7
What's Wrong with My Current Retirement Financial Plan?

After reading this far, you might be feeling somewhat manipulated. The less financial knowledge you have, the more likely it is that you might feel this way. The good news is that now is always the best time to address a bad situation, and this book provides you with the tools to take control of your financial future.

But you are worried! "I don't really want to take on the risk of investing in the stock market at my age. I can't afford the losses!"

The financial institutions are well aware of this natural human tendency, and they know exactly how to take advantage of it!

People tend to overestimate short-term risks while underestimating long-term ones. Additionally, we often assume that something that is low risk now will remain low risk over the long term.

At my favourite bank a few years ago, my risk profile was based on my age, my current financial worth, and one question – "Do you like risk?" Risk is a complex concept. Understanding its nature is one of the most crucial lessons in achieving success in your financial life.

To compare the simple risk component of my bank's personal financial planning process, as a licensed independent financial consultant, I know that the risk discussion during an initial consultation with a new client takes at least 10 minutes, even if the client understands all the concepts. There are many nuances to be grasped in this area to fully comprehend a client's needs. For most small investors, the total appointment time for a first meeting with the lowest-level investment "specialist" at your local bank is just 12.5 minutes!

My risk profile at my financial institution would have been the average risk profile of an uninformed person of my age, had I not insisted that I was well informed and understood the components of total risk. A simple question that could have been asked to better understand me would have been: "How well do you understand personal financial management and the operation of financial markets?"

So, the bank's process is designed to arbitrarily lower my risk profile, which would have forced me into lower-performing asset classes than those I wanted for my long-term investment. What's required to combat this tendency is your knowledge of basic financial concepts!

All this may seem bad enough, but you should also know that the bank is naturally incentivized to keep client risk profiles as low as possible. If the branch can get me into the low-risk category, my money will go into GICs. The bank's profit from these is huge!

How profitable is my GIC to the bank? A quick recap of what we saw in the last chapter.

Find the mortgage rate for the same time frame as the GIC you are considering. Currently, the 5-year GIC rate is 4.5%, while the 5-year mortgage rate is 5.5%. Multiply that mortgage rate by 20, and that's the gross return the bank generates from your money. Yes, that's 110% per year! Much higher than credit card rates, which are already significantly greater than the banks' cost of money!

Certainly, there are expenses associated with generating that return. The bank must pay the 4.5% on my GIC!

You may hear people at the branch saying that there are also the expenses incurred in running the branch. That's the purpose of your monthly account fees — to cover the cost of the branches. There are costs related to the bank's mortgage operations department and a few other overhead charges. However, none of this changes the fact that GICs are extremely profitable for the banks.

Clearly, the bank wants your investments in a plan with a risk profile as low as possible. What about you? Do you want this?

Assets in the form of money or interest-bearing securities are low risk in the short term but carry higher total risk in the long term due to inflation and the risk of asset depletion. This asset class includes all types of cash accounts at a bank, GICs, money market funds, T-Bills, and short-term debts (30, 90, and 180-day). With these asset classes generating returns below the rate of inflation, your purchasing power decreases every year. There's little chance of growing a large enough pool to retire comfortably, no matter the age at which a person starts saving.

Is that a risk you'd be willing to take?

Unless you have a few million dollars available now to fund your retirement, you'll need a return higher than the rate of inflation to retire comfortably.

However, as we've seen, most financial institutions typically recommend only low-risk plans for those who have retired or are nearing retirement.

The critical step for anyone looking to get more from their retirement is to either find an independent advisor you can trust or take an active role in managing your finances across two or three financial institutions. Just a reminder: when we say "independent advisor," we mean an advisor who isn't tied to a company that markets its own products. For the "non-independent advisor," there's always an incentive to steer you toward specific products that the company wants to promote. These are always the products that generate the most profit for the company and, as a result, may not be the ones that generate the most profit for you.

Consumer surveys show that having access to truly independent financial advice is strongly correlated with long-term investor success!

The next chapter outlines what you need to do to integrate these assets into your portfolio to significantly improve your retirement cash flow!

Chapter 8
Fixing My Retirement Plan

You might still be worried! "I don't know what to do to drive a better retirement lifestyle!"

Here's where we revisit the fifth assumption your financial institution makes about you, as outlined in Chapter 1—another narrative pushed by the financial industry. This assumption is that financial planning is overly complex, with math that is beyond the comprehension of most Canadians.

In reality, it's NOT COMPLICATED!

That's right! There is no advanced math required to manage your personal financial future. Simplifications, such as the Rule of 72, effectively remove much of the complexity involved in professional portfolio management.

All the math you need to manage your financial future, you knew by the end of grade 7!

Why weren't we given class problems that would show us how to achieve financial independence?

Because then you would become independent!

So, let's look at how we can better manage our retirement.

What we want is to increase the returns on our assets while lowering the overall level of risk exposure in our total portfolio. We can achieve this by aligning our assets with the timing of the cash flow we desire. But before we dive into how to do that, let's review a few key concepts from Parts 1 and 2.

As mentioned in previous chapters, assets in the form of money or interest-bearing securities are low risk in the short term but carry higher overall risk in the long term due to inflation and the risk of asset depletion. Since these asset classes typically generate returns below the rate of inflation, it's unlikely that they will grow into a pool large enough to support a reasonable retirement lifestyle, no matter when someone starts saving. Achieving this would require a significant amount of money.

Bonds are lower risk if held to maturity, but carry higher risk if sold before maturity. The actual risk level of a bond also depends significantly on the creditworthiness of the borrower. Most mutual funds that invest across multiple bond classes are rated as Medium Low risk.

Funds that invest in dividend-paying stocks are also typically Medium Low risk, although they carry slightly more risk than bond funds. In years when the stock market declines, these funds tend to fall less because the dividends provide a base for the stock's value. Due to preferential tax treatment, dividend payouts are more favourable than interest income. This preference makes these funds less likely to experience losses in consecutive years. Over a two-to-three-year period, these funds usually offer a return slightly higher than inflation.

The stock market as a whole is very risky in the short term but much less risky over the long term – particularly over periods of more than 6 years. Many of the best-performing mutual funds in the long term are stock-only funds that follow the investing strategy discussed in Chapter 3. These funds generally invest with a 5-year horizon, so you should be prepared to hold them for at least that long. Stock-based mutual funds range from Medium through Medium High to High and Speculative risk levels. Mutual funds that specialize in subsets of the total market tend to have higher risk, as do those that invest in smaller companies or raw materials like mining. Funds that buy dividend-paying stocks generally have lower risk ratings.

Hopefully, you're now thinking, "Surely it must be possible to combine these assets to significantly improve my retirement cash flow at a reasonable total risk?" If so, give yourself another gold star for staying ahead of me! Sadly, you would be wrong – again! Your institution cannot allow you to invest in assets with a higher financial risk rating than your plan permits! You can't get there from here... or can you?

To change your financial future, you only need to alter one assumption from where you are now! If you recall, once your income becomes limited, and you'll need to withdraw funds from your savings within the next 3 to 5 years, every financial institution is required to ensure you have a low-risk plan to cover the short-term need for funds!

So, what do you do? Simple!

You need more than 1 financial plan! In fact, you'll need 3!

In this chapter, we'll present the steps to put your new plans into place. In the next chapter, we'll provide examples of total 3-Plan performance.

The first step in planning for your retirement is to determine the monthly cost of the lifestyle you want to maintain. When calculating your monthly budget, consider the costs for the upcoming month, without factoring in inflation. To sustain that lifestyle, you must cover your expenses each month, increasing annually at the inflation rate.

This budget of expenses must be covered by incoming cash flow. In retirement, you cash flow will come from several potential sources including:

1. Government pension and income support programs

2. Company pension plans

3. Income from casual work

4. Rental income

5. Cash from investments.

Add up all the known sources of monthly incoming cash and subtract that from the budgeted expenses. The remaining amount is the monthly cash you need from your investments.

Your short-term plan will cover this need for 24 months. To be cautious, we'll fund this plan as if it will generate no investment income, even though your short-term money will be invested in GICs or money market funds, depending on your risk profile and the products available through your chosen advisor. Multiply the monthly cash flow requirement by 24. That's the initial amount for your short-term plan.

The 3 – Plan Retirement TM

The medium-term plan is designed to provide the cash flow for years 3 through 6. That's 48 months, so multiply 48 by your monthly cash requirements for this plan. A typical risk profile for this plan might be 50 to 100% Medium-Low and 0 to 50% Medium risk. The investments in this plan include funds that invest in bonds and dividend-paying stocks.

As we indicated above, these funds tend to return a bit more than inflation, so the initial investment should, on average, grow by more than inflation.

The remainder of your funds will go into the long-term plan. This plan should be split between Medium and Medium-High risks. Remember that the stock market index is considered Medium Risk. This plan is invested in growth funds, with a time horizon of five years or longer for the investments within the fund.

The specific funds you select for your plan should provide superior returns over 5 and 10 years. You should ignore 1 and 3-year returns for this plan, as the market goes through cycles in which different types of stocks grow (or decline) at a higher rate than others. Some funds may look better in the short term if their investment style has been in vogue in recent years. Over the full market cycle – typically 7 years or longer – these "in fashion" differences tend to level out. This means that longer-term results better measure the ability of the fund managers.

Another important consideration when selecting funds is whether the fund managers have been with the fund for the full 10 years. If a newer fund manager is in place, I wouldn't recommend investing in that fund. Let someone else take the risk of a fund manager establishing a performance record. The only exception to this rule is if there's another fund with excellent performance that the new manager has overseen for the entire 10-year period.

To reiterate, we are recommending mutual funds because the average person does not have the time to properly manage their investments and should therefore rely on professionals with a strong track record. The results you see when your advisor shows you the fund's datasheet are the net results you would have received after all fees for fund management have been subtracted. This means that you don't need to worry about the costs of the fund, only the returns that the manager delivers!

That's all there is to implementing the 3-Plan Retirement™. No challenging math, other than preparing a monthly budget!

But there is some work to be done at the start of every year. Annually, we must replenish the money we have withdrawn each month from the short-term plan, ensuring that our plan remains free of short-term market concerns. That money will come from the medium-term fund.

How much will we transfer between funds? We want our cash flow to increase each year at the rate of inflation, so that our purchasing power does not decrease, as is typical with most fixed-income retirement plans. Multiply your monthly cash flow from the previous year by the rate of inflation. Take that new monthly cash flow and multiply it by 24. That's the amount of money you want in your short-term plan at the start of the new year. Transfer the difference between the amount you want and the amount you currently have in the account.

Once this first transfer is complete, the medium-term plan is likely to be underfunded. To calculate how much this fund needs to be fully funded, multiply the new monthly cash flow by 48 to get the target funding level. If this amount is lower than the current balance in the fund, transfer the difference from the long-term fund.

Ask your advisor to adjust your new cash flow level, then sit back and enjoy another year. That's the entire 3-Plan structure and operation! There may be reasons to make some adjustments, but we'll discuss those in the next chapter.

How well does the 3-Plan methodology work? That's next!

Chapter 9
Result Scenarios

There are five interacting variables in the 3-Plan Retirement™ portfolios. To evaluate the potential results of the 3-Plan Retirement™, we will assume values for four of these variables and present the outcome of the fifth in the final column of each table below. As we progress through this chapter, we will change one variable at a time. This approach is designed to help you understand the risks involved in the overall 3-Plan portfolio.

For these examples, we will use a single return rate for each of the 3-Plans. Since it's important that you feel comfortable with your investments, the rates used will be somewhat conservative. It's unlikely that the returns of any of the three plans will match these rates in any given year, so the scenarios presented will reflect an average value. At the end of this chapter, we will discuss possible modifications to the plan if the markets experience either an exceptional or poor year.

The variables in the plan are:

1) Initial capital. We will use $100,000 as the initial amount to simplify the calculation, allowing for easy multiplication based on the size of your investment assets. To estimate your cash flow, simply multiply the examples by the size of your current portfolio and divide by 100,000.

2) Monthly cashflow requirements. For your convenience, we will also quote the percentage of the initial capital that would be paid out in the first year at the given monthly cash flow. Remember, this cash flow increases annually by the rate of inflation.

3) Investment returns for the short-term, medium-term and long-term investment plans.

4) The underlying inflation rate.

5) The number of years until the plans are depleted and the cash flow stops.

Remember, inflation adjustments are incorporated into all these scenarios. If the underlying inflation rate is 3% (which is above the Bank of Canada's target), then by year 25, the monthly cash flow of $583 (taken from line one of the first table) would need to increase to $1,186 to maintain the same purchasing power.

How Long Will The Money Last?

The first question we will explore is "How long will my $100k last?" Our base case assumes 4% short-term returns, 8% for the medium-term funds, and 10% for the long-term investments, with a 7% payout ratio. This is shown in row 1. All other rows demonstrate how changes to any of the listed variables impact the overall performance.

Row	Inflation Rate	Short-term return	Medium-term return	Long-term return	Monthly cashflow	Years until money runs out
1	3	4	8	10	583 (7% annual)	25
2	3	2	8	10	583 (7% annual)	24.5
3	3	4	8	12	583 (7% annual)	40
4	3	4	8	12	750 (9% annual)	17
5	3	4	7	10	583 (7% annual)	24
6	3	4	7	12	583 (7% annual)	37
7	3	4	8	10	750 (9% annual)	14.8
8	3	4	8	12	750 (9% annual)	16.5

The 3 – Plan Retirement TM

9	4	4	8	10	583 (7% annual)	21

Comparing rows 1 and 2 in the table shows that the short-term interest rate has little effect on how long the money will last. Reducing the short-term rate from 4% in row 1 to 2% in row 2 cuts the payout period by just 6 months over 25 years.

The third row increases the long-term return to 12%, compared to row 1. At a 7% annual payout, this plan lasts for 40 years! However, if we increase the annual payout to 9% (as shown in row 4), the plan will last only 17 years. Comparing row 3 to row 1, we can see that long-term returns have a significant impact on your plan's results. We'll explore this further in a later scenario.

Lowering the medium-term return, as shown in rows 5 and 6, shortens the plan's payout period by 14 to 16 months at the 7% payout and by almost 3 years at the 12% return with a 9% payout. Compare rows 5 and 1, as well as rows 6 and 3.

Increasing the annual payout rate, as seen when comparing row 7 to row 1 and row 8 to row 3, significantly shortens the time the fund continues to pay out its inflation-adjusted monthly cashflow.

Comparing rows 1 and 9, we observe that inflation can also have a significant impact on fund performance. Adding just 1% to the average long-term inflation reduces a 25-year payout to just 21 years.

Summarizing the results, the impacts on your plans from these variables, ranked from greatest to least, are the long-term returns, the payout ratio, the inflation rate, the medium-term return, and the short-term return. Since you can't control the inflation rate, it's essential to focus on the performance of the long-term investments when deciding how to invest your funds.

How Much Money Can I Get?

The second most commonly asked question is "How much money can I take out if I want the plan to last 25 years?"

Inflation Rate	Short-term return	Medium-term return	Long-term return	Monthly cashflow (annual rate)
3	3	8	10	583 (7.0%)
3	3	8	12	633 (7.6%)
4	3	8	10	580 (7.0%)
4	3	8	12	635 (7.6%)
3	3	7	10	571 (6.9%)
3	3	7	12	621 (7.5%)
3	4	8	10	589 (7.1%)
3	4	8	12	641 (7.7%)

This table enables you to determine your initial monthly cash flow based on your accumulated retirement funds and the assumptions you've made. Compare odd-numbered rows to Row 1 and even-numbered rows to Row 2. The net results are consistent with those of the first table: the primary factor influencing your cash flow is the performance of the long-term funds.

What Return Do I Need?

Our final question asks, "What is the long-term rate needed to provide monthly cashflow for the specified number of years?" To simplify the table, we will fix most of the variables. The initial investment is $100,000, with a 3% short-term return and an 8% medium-term return. Inflation will be set at 3%

The 3 – Plan Retirement TM

Initial Monthly Cashflow	Rate for 15 years of cashflow	Rate for 25 years of cashflow	Rate for 35 years of cashflow	Rate for 50 years of cashflow
$583 - 7%	3%	10%	11.9%	12.5%
$667 - 8%	6.2%	13.4%	14.6%	15.05%
$750 - 9%	11.1%	16.9%	17.85%	18.1%
10%	16.0%	21.0%	21.65%	21.8%

As an example of how to read this table, if my target were to draw cash for 35 years at a first-year withdrawal rate of 8% of my initial investment, adjusted annually for inflation, then the long-term investments would need to achieve an average return of 14.6% over those 35 years.

Before we discuss how we might achieve these growth rates, take note of how little additional return is required to extend the viability of our plan from 25 years to 50 years! This is the true power of compound growth!

Is This Realistic?

Throughout these scenarios, we have been using 10% and 12% as our long-term returns. These correspond to the longer-term results from the S&P 500 index and the NASDAQ over 60 years. Many of the returns in the previous table are much larger than these rates! Are they realistic?

Let's look back at the 2010s as a decade. The highest mutual fund return for the entire decade in a Medium-High risk fund was just over 30% per year, compounded!

Even after a challenging 2022 market, there are currently at least 20 Canadian mutual funds in the Medium or Medium-High risk categories that have a 10-year performance exceeding the 21.8% level. So, this level of performance is achievable.

But you shouldn't base your retirement plans on achieving such returns – which is why we used average market returns in the earlier scenarios. Instead, we should treat higher returns as a bonus.

How should we react to such high gains?

My recommendation would be to do nothing until the long-term fund can cover this year's annual transfer to the Medium-term fund by generating only an 8% return this year. At that point, you will have a few options.

1) Take a lump sum from the long-term fund for a major purchase or a gift to family members. Always ensure there is enough money left to cover the annual transfer, assuming a 10% return this year.

2) Reduce the overall risk of your 3-Plans by transferring an additional year's worth of monthly cashflow into the Medium-term fund, and moving three months of that addition into the short-term funds.

3) My preference would be to increase your monthly cashflow by 10%, which would require transferring slightly less than in option 2—2.4 months of additional cash into the short-term fund, compared to the 3 months in option 2.

Your advisor may have additional suggestions and can help you analyze any other ideas you want to consider.

What if the markets fell in the past year?

As you saw in the scenarios above, the long-term return is the primary driver of your plans' performance. Ideally, you should leave enough money in the long-term fund to cover the next year's transfer to the medium-term fund, assuming the long-term fund returns 12%. Most good growth funds do not experience two bad years in a row, and typically, a bad year is followed by a strong one! Once your funds have a strong year, make up the difference in the medium-term fund so that it fully covers the 48-month payout at the current monthly cash flow level.

The criteria I use for selecting the medium-term funds I offer my clients include ensuring the fund manager has a positive return over every 3-year period during which they've managed the fund. Such a record will ensure that the medium-term fund does not lose all its money before being fully replenished by the growth in the long-term fund.

Thus, the medium-term fund serves as a buffer in your plan. The plan will still work even if the medium-term fund drops to half its target level at the end of each year. This will only occur with two consecutive years of down markets.

Chapter 10
When to Start

The 3-Plan Retirement™ concept presented in this book offers an excellent model for lifelong investment portfolio management, with one major exception.

A good financial adviser should align your investments with the financial goals you provide. Goals expected to be achieved within 2 years should be funded by investments with lower risk. Goals expected to be achieved within 6 years should be invested in defensive equity and bond funds, while goals that are more than 6 years away should be funded by growth-oriented funds.

In general, you should have an emergency fund that covers 3 to 6 months of income available in case you suddenly lose your current source of income. The number of months covered depends on your ability to withstand risk and your estimate of how long it might take to restore your income.

A medium-term investment could be used if you plan to buy a car in a few years. If you lease a vehicle, those expenses should be covered by your income this year, not by your investments. Similarly, most vacations should be funded by this year's income. However, a bucket-list vacation planned several years in advance would likely rely on a medium-term investment until the last year before the vacation.

The one major exception? Buying a new home – especially for first-time buyers. House and condo prices, on average, rise faster than the interest rates paid by short-term investments. Saving for a home purchase using short-term investments will significantly lengthen the time required to save, unless home prices are expected to fall this year.

It's extremely difficult to predict the price performance of any housing market for the next year, as both supply and demand can be quickly impacted by events unrelated to the price of housing. Variables that impact home prices include interest rates, growth in the overall economy, the financial health of large employers in your area, changes in weather patterns, and natural disasters. Most people making predictions begin with the national economy and consider that, about 90% of the time, home prices rise annually.

This is only a quick overview of the considerations required when deciding how to save for your home purchase. Clearly, there are risks you should consider as you approach the time to make a major purchase, such as a home.

What about retirement planning?

To follow the 3-Plan Retirement™ model, you should start to arrange your financial assets 6 years before you retire.

At this point, your first step is to estimate the monthly cash flow you'll need from your investments. Multiply this number by 11 and transfer that amount of money from your long-term investments to medium-term investments.

Why 11? We begin transferring money 6 full years before retirement, allowing it to grow in the intervening years. Alternatively, wait until 5 years before retirement, then transfer 12 times the monthly required cash flow.

Continue with whichever process you choose annually until 1 year prior to retirement. At this point, transfer 12 times the monthly required cash flow to a short-term account – probably a 365-day GIC or money market investment.

Finally, upon retirement transfer an additional 12 months to the short-term investment portfolio, and you're ready to go.

People whose retirement plans suffered the most during the 2008 and 2022 market downturns were typically those who had all their money in riskier long-term investments, seeking the larger returns that these types of investments historically provided in the years leading up to a market crash.

Be disciplined in following this plan, or whichever plan you feel best suits your retirement goals. The purpose of the 3-Plan Retirement™

model is to reduce overall life risk in your financial portfolios. For those who are close to retirement, there may not be enough time to recover from a bad market year if all their money is invested in long-term funds.

Defensive stocks fell by about 25% in 2008, while long-term growth stocks dropped nearly 50%. Both had fully recovered their losses by the end of 2011, but the short-term need for cash in 2009, 2010, and 2011 could have severely impacted your retirement plans if you had kept all your investments in the higher-risk categories.

Chapter 11
Summary

The 3-Plan model can increase your lifestyle without significantly increasing the financial risk of your portfolio. The 3-Plan Retirement™ plan presented here substantially boosts your initial cashflow and provides inflation protection.

Because of the short-term plan, you have lower exposure to the market and are mostly independent of short-term market fluctuations.

Yes, the plan DOES depend on the stock market rising in the medium and long terms. Historically, relying on the market over this time frame has worked out well. However, there are always enterprising individuals with products and ideas to sell, who know that fear drives people to buy more than desire does. These individuals constantly make predictions of doom, increasing fear among those who don't fully understand how the stock market works.

Only a small portion of a company's stocks are traded in the open market. Most are held by large investors and mutual funds. Over half the value of the US stock markets is controlled by 1% of the population. For these individuals, the stock market is not even half of their investments. They also invest in real estate, bonds, private equity, art, collectibles, and other assets. Despite having the resources to buy 100% of the listed stocks in the stock market, they don't. Why?

For them, the stock market is an excellent way to take easy money from people who don't understand how to properly invest. We are easy targets because we don't fully grasp the rules of the game. We become emotional about the market, and that is the worst thing we can do.

When the wealthy believe the market has risen enough, they slowly begin selling off a small percentage of their holdings. The excess supply of stocks drives the price of those stocks down. Done on a broad scale, the entire market starts to decline. Within a few weeks, a landslide effect takes hold, even though the wealthy have stopped selling by then.

The downward trend continues, accelerating as panic selling by smaller retail investors begins. These individuals believe the downtrend will persist, and that they will lose their entire financial future if they don't sell now.

With everyone selling, the wealthy begin accumulating shares once more, buying back the shares they sold months earlier to push the market down. They are purchasing these shares at a much lower price than they sold them for, locking in their profits at the expense of those who bought high and sold low!

Some market insiders, monitoring the situation, recognize that the wealthy are buying again, and they join in. As a result, the market rises rapidly. Meanwhile, retail investors still believe the market will fall further, while the insiders rake in large profits. Almost all the biggest gains in the market occur shortly after the bottom, with retail investors left on the sidelines. Missing these significant gains results in those who try to time the market only achieving half the long-term gains of those who stayed invested.

This is the truth of the market axiom "It's not TIMING the market, but TIME IN the market that determines your results".

Be courageous and allow the financial system to work its magic, knowing that you have 3-Plans in place, each maximizing returns with appropriate risks across short, medium, and long-term time frames.

More cash flow each month leads to a better life for most Canadians. You, too, can enjoy a better life!

Epilog

Recently, I had my first interaction with Canada's new regulator for the investment industry. The Canadian Investment Regulatory Organization (CIRO) began operations on January 3, 2023, following a year-long planning process. CIRO takes over from several regulatory bodies in the investment industry, representing a significant opportunity to enhance the consistency of operations across the sector and help us increase our focus on client service. I have been very hopeful about the potential improvements this will bring.

Here are a few excerpts from CIRO documents which encourage me.

"CIRO is carrying on the regulatory functions of the Investment Industry Regulatory Organization of Canada and the Mutual Fund Dealers Association of Canada, and is committed to the protection of investors, providing efficient and consistent regulation, and building Canadians' trust in financial regulation and the people managing their investments."

Excerpt from the CIRO website.

"For years prior to CIRO's creation on January 1, 2023, there were concerns about how the then-existing system of the Mutual Fund Dealers Association and the Investment Industry Regulatory Organization of Canada, operating as two parallel SROs, wasn't efficient enough, maintained regulatory silos which made the industry less effective and, most importantly, prevented Canadians from obtaining financial services and financial advice in the ways they wanted and needed."

From the introduction to CIRO's first Strategic Plan

"Finally, it is important to underline again our role as a self-regulatory organization which operates in the public interest. To us, that means we work together with the industry we regulate, together with the markets we oversee, together with our CSA partners and most importantly together with the Canadians whose financial futures we protect."

From the introduction to CIRO's first Strategic Plan

CIRO's Vision is:

Be an agile and trusted regulator. Who helps the investment industry deliver the right financial outcomes for investors.

The Mission Statement is:

Promote healthy capital markets by regulating fairly and effectively so that investors feel protected and confident investing for their futures.

I also think highly of the Corporate Values and the process by which CIRO employees developed these.

We Do What is Right

- We treat everyone with respect.

- We are open and transparent.

We Foster Inclusion

- We embrace diversity and recognize our differences can be our greatest asset to fuel innovation and growth.

We are Effective

- We believe in and are accountable for our important work.

- We endeavour to go above and beyond.

We are Forward Thinking

- We leverage innovative technologies to stay ahead of the curve.

- We celebrate those taking the initiative.

There is much here to feel positive about.

I am slightly concerned that "the Canadians whose financial futures we protect" is not clearly defined. However, the working definition seems to be "people who interact in any way with CIRO members." I also note that some subsidiaries of Canada's banks are CIRO members, but the branches themselves are not.

We must be aware that when investing through the branches, we may not be protected by CIRO policies. It's important to ask first, before making any investments.

Once again, I'm hopeful for better days ahead for Canadians, particularly working-class and middle-class investors, for whom the current system has not been as helpful as it could have been.

However, as noted above, I recently had my first interaction with CIRO, and I'm a bit concerned—enough so to include a summary of the interaction thus far in this book. I find it highly instructive as to the actual purpose of CIRO, which seems to differ from what was stated— protecting the financial futures of Canadians!

If it hasn't become clear in this book, my belief is that financial futures are best protected when investors achieve the best risk-adjusted returns for their money. We need our hard-earned money to work equally hard for us.

I met a new prospective client in September 2022, referred by an existing client. After three meetings, during which I outlined the 3-plan model from this book, the prospect agreed to become a client. I explained that the worst possible outcome would be if the market declined significantly in the first year, but that this did not seem likely after the recent market turndown. Nevertheless, we decided to fund the short-term plan with four years of monthly cash payments, and the client opted for a lower monthly cash amount than the plan would allow. This is ideal for investors with high risk aversion.

I normally charge a 3% commission whenever a client deposits money into an account. This covers my knowledge and services, along with approximately 0.5% of the asset value as an annual trailer. As explained earlier, trailers are beneficial for an investor's accounts because they incentivize the agent to find the best possible ways to grow the account, which also increases the agent's income.

Since the funds the new client would be investing exceeded the trigger level I use, the client was offered a discounted rate of 2.5%. This was implemented as no commission for the short-term plan, and 3% for the medium- and long-term plans. All funds used were Medium Risk or lower. The short-term plan was entirely invested in money market funds.

The market has performed well since the investments were made. The client increased the monthly cashflow to the recommended level after six months, once they saw the funds performing well.

At the time of writing, the client has withdrawn almost 10% of the original capital as monthly cash flow. This aligns with the 7% example provided earlier. The client's remaining capital in the investment accounts has grown by just over 30%, even after "paying back" my commission. Truly, a success story!

So, I was shocked to receive the following from the company which manages my agency and my client accounts.

"There was inadequate documentation to support the suitability determination to purchase funds with a 3% Front End sales charge and demonstrate that the client's interests were put first considering other available alternatives"

Since I had documented the conversations with the client, I sent a note to our compliance team asking why they didn't simply forward that to CIRO. The reply was that CIRO wanted to know WHY I charged 3% — the documentation was fine. In other words, CIRO wanted to understand how I set my base pricing.

A few thoughts here…

1) CIRO was asking me why I took the actions I did at a time in the past before CIRO existed. Although the investigation determined that no rules were broken, CIRO seem to believe their standards should be applied backwards in time.

2) Independent advisors sell mutual funds either on an up-front commission basis or an annual fee. The net income to the agent is usually similar either way. No independent agents are paid a

salary, except for certain companies that offer an "advance" on future commission earnings to help a new agent get started in the business. New agents often struggle with lower incomes, much like entrepreneurs building a new business. Working in financial services is not an easy career path, as it takes time to build up income streams — either fees or commissions.

3) How people set their prices in any industry is a matter of supply and demand. The legal range for Front-End charges, as stated elsewhere in this book, is anywhere from 0% to 5%. A significant majority of my clients (and all who have stayed with me for four or more years) achieve outstanding results compared to their friends, so they refer me to those willing to consider my investment style. Regulators and bureaucrats should not be concerned with anyone operating within the legal parameters set by the regulator monitoring the market at the time of the transaction.

4) Other than the two types of independent agents (commission-based and fee-based), the only other model in use in the financial services industry is to pay agents a salary. This is the model used in bank branches. I have two basic concerns with using the bank model as my investment partner. The first is that the agent does not care how my investment performs, whereas an independent agent does, precisely because it drives long-term compensation for the agent. The second concern is that the people the bank uses to handle investments for smaller clients are not incentivized to learn about other products that might interest the client, other than those the bank asks them to know. Many of these individuals are not actually licensed and must rely on the recommendations of the computer system provided to guide them. Not surprisingly, these people change jobs (and employers) frequently, as they are educated and have higher aspirations that involve independent thinking in their roles.

5) Thinking about the CLIENT's interests involves achieving returns for that CLIENT that are among the best available at the

given risk level of the investments. It's NOT about lowering commissions to the point where independent agents are driven out of the business due to an inability to earn a reasonable income during the first five years or so of their career in the financial industry. The idea that CIRO would target a 2.5% total commission on a portfolio that has generated almost 40% over 18 months, after deducting my commissions, leaves me somewhat incredulous.

6) As mentioned earlier in the discussion about discount brokers, the average small investor is not well served when working with cost-focused individuals. A recent survey found that almost all customers who don't spend at least 15 hours a week on their investments with discount brokerages lose most of their money. This is precisely why we pay independent agents—to handle this work on our behalf. We must learn to focus on net returns AFTER costs, not just on the costs themselves. CIRO should be investigating how to educate Canadians on this basic truth.

One final thought that occurred to me while working through this issue (which is not yet fully resolved) is that the actions of CIRO in this case, if continued over the long term, would eventually push all independent agents out of the business. It creates a greater workload for the agent, not the efficiency that aligns with the core Values of CIRO. This would be a major boon for the bank branches, leaving them with no competition for your investment dollar.

What can you do?

Be informed and don't be afraid to speak with your federal politician – who likely has enough income to be well served by the financial system – just not at a bank branch!